AF324673

SPEAKING OUT

SPEAKING OUT

REVIEWING THE SCHOOL SUSPENSION POLICY

JONATHAN BECKETT

ACADEMICA PRESS
LONDON-WASHINGTON

Library of Congress Cataloguing-in-Publication Data

Names: Beckett, Jonathan.
Title: Speaking out : reviewing school suspension policy / Jonathan Beckett.
Description: London ; Washington : Academia Press, [2017] | Includes
  bibliographical references and index.
Identifiers: LCCN 2017046880 | ISBN 9781680530469
Subjects: LCSH: Student suspension--Great Britain.
Classification: LCC LB3089.4.G7 B43 2017 | DDC 371.5/43--dc23
LC record available at https://lccn.loc.gov/2017046880

Academica Press
1727 Massachusetts Avenue, NW, Suite 507
Washington, DC 20036
academicapress.editorial@gmail.com

For orders call
(978) 829-2577

CONTENTS

PREFACE

This work is a critical evaluative investigation into developing and re-writing a whole school policy for school exclusion. It will use the findings of this work to re-structure the existing policy and clarify when exclusion may be considered an appropriate course of action in dealing with severe inappropriate behaviour. In so doing this work aims to 'sharpen' the focus of the school exclusion policy to give specific instances of when exclusion may be executed. Moreover, it will use interview schedule data to reflect upon the emotional and physical response exclusion can create, which will help to consider the use of exclusion in the light of these matters.

This book critically assesses the usefulness of biographical research when considering the nature, feature and characteristics of school exclusion. Moreover, it notes from government guidance the specific nature of school exclusion, what it is and when it may be applied. It also identifies research findings of professional bodies which cite examples of when exclusion has been implemented. I consider the characteristics of an exclusion and address potential problems, such as child care issues, in which a child is excluded and no parent is available to look after them. This may also form a potential barrier between the school and the student. Problems for the school in implementing an exclusion are considered in the light of literature and research, such as the overturning of headteacher's decisions by governors or independent appeals panels.

Against this background the book notes how professional practice can be developed by interviewing students and staff about school exclusion. The project focuses upon reviewing the school exclusion policy within a Primary school in Hampshire. By interviewing students, the perspective of what it is like to receive an exclusion can be ascertained. This meant that I was able to find out about how individuals felt about being excluded. Additionally, the interviews illumined how staff felt in relation to the process, such as were they supportive of exclusion or did they consider another course of action more appropriate? This project has highlighted a number of original issues which have been explored in this book. Through this type of research, policies have been developed, professional practice explored and action taken as a result of the impact this work has had upon educational practice.

Chapter 1 Introduction

1.1 Introducing the research enquiry

This work has been designed to critically reflect upon a current educational issue within the school I work. The research focuses upon reviewing the current school exclusion policy. At present the policy is viewed as antiquated and does not reflect current practice. The policy is currently unclear and is not specific enough for the purpose it was designed for, which was clarity of understanding of what exclusion is, when it may be used appropriately and its implications for all those involved.

This book addresses the impact of educational practice within the scope of the issue of school exclusion through biographical research. Thus, I seek to identify the nature and distinguishing features involved in the exclusion process. In so doing the work will look at what is meant by 'school exclusion', the grounds on which an exclusion was made and the impact of it upon those involved in the process. Moreover, critical discussion of how biographical research can be used to highlight the experiences of those who have been excluded and the impact that this has had upon their cognitive and psychological development. This project is particularly pertinent and timely as it is important to have a greater understanding of school exclusion to direct and govern policy and to develop an appreciation of the impact of exclusion on those involved in the process. Through this professional practice can be informed and adjustments be made, where required.

The rationale for this research is that listening to the learner is important to me as a practitioner, something which Flutter and Ruddock (2004) advocate. To set the scene locally, I have decided to interview students from a school in which I work in Hampshire. This school is located outside of Basingstoke in an area of moderate to high social deprivation. According to a previous Ofsted inspection report, the number of students receiving free school meals is slightly higher than average. The current rate of school exclusion is higher than some similar schools, within the local catchment area. The school is currently reviewing many different policies and the exclusion one is to be altered as a result of pupil consultation and the outcomes of this work. This is because the headteacher and I believe that the students are more likely to respond to rules they have mutually agreed and policies they have had an input into. Cowley (2003) stresses this point, that if students are engaged in making and understanding the rules and expectations they are more likely to keep them. By way of setting the scene nationally, trends and statistics of exclusion give indicators of the prevalence of exclusion. From analysing statistics from the 1990s exclusion rates, there was a peak in the number of students excluded between 1992 and 1997 (Gordon, 2001). However, the occurrences of exclusion have decreased according to more recent quantitative data in the years following. However, have peaked again in the period of this work up to 2017 (see Appendix 1). It is not the purpose of this work to analyse numerical data, such as statistics as the scope of this work is based upon biographical qualitative research.

As the primary focus of this work I shall interview those who have experienced exclusion from school and ask them for their feelings about this. The reason for doing so is to allow these individuals a voice to share their experiences (Forde et al. 2006). From past research at Bachelor's and Master's level I have noted some individuals feel oppressed and unable to give their viewpoint within a system they are may be fighting (Nind et al. 2003). Therefore, this work has been developed out of a keen interest into school exclusion as well as the desire to promote, as Moon (2004) notes, open consultation with students. Furthermore, as Gerver (2010) identifies as a priority, this work draws upon practitioners' viewpoints in relation to exclusion, asking staff what they think about exclusion as a sanction. This is particularly important as it offers teachers and other staff an opening to share their opinion and offer their perspective upon exclusion. This research is embedded within professional practice -aiming for generalisability - using the notion of consultation to inform me and others about student and staff perceptions of exclusion. It asks: how effective is exclusion as a sanction?

What do staff and students think about it? Once I have obtained this data I can work with other senior staff to revise the exclusion policy.

Within the book I will outline the beneficial implications as well as the limitations of using interviews as a biographical research method to explore professional practice in relation to school exclusion. This work specifically focuses upon the rich data that can be obtained through a willing participant's responses (Harris and Passmore 2009). It is especially important that this work identifies, as Goodley (2001) argues, that students do not feel coerced into participating if they do not wish to, particularly in the light of perceived power issues between staff and student. I shall mention how I explain to potential participants that I am to be seen as a 'researcher' rather than a 'teacher' and they are at liberty to not give consent, without feeling that this will have a detrimental impact upon them. Thus, within this book I make clear that any volunteer is given a briefing before agreeing to be interviewed and that all participants have the opportunity to not participate or withdraw at any time, without reason. The draw backs of such approaches are that when students are interviewed, the existence of power relationships may be present (Hobbs 2005). Moreover, this book argues this can lead to distorted responses being obtained and subsequently underlines the importance of I creating a rapport which contributes to open and honest interaction. In terms of analysis, Erben (1998) advocates that pertinent events, the context of these events and the societal context and documentary evidence should be considered when making a biographical analysis. Erben's work also suggests that imagination should be incorporated within the analysis of data. Gedo and Gedo (1992) further emphasise the importance of creativity in research design, analysis and interpretation. The effect of school exclusion, viewed biographically, can be analysed through key note events that occur from the respondents' answers.

As biographical research is primarily a qualitative research tool taking into account the lived experiences, I suggest that quantitative data, although useful in analysing prevalence and specific instances of exclusion, has limitations when addressing the nature, characteristics and the interpretation of school exclusion (Simons 2010). Furthermore, I explain as MacBeath and

Myers (1999) do so, from a biographical stance the potential problems that school leaders may face in the implementation of the exclusion process. For example, if appeals against permanent exclusion are successful, reintegration may be problematic for the child and the school. Another area specifically drawn upon by Cooper (2002) is how exclusion may have detrimental effects upon the excluded and their families. Thus, from a narrative research perspective the book looks at alternatives to exclusion such as: effective sanction systems, positive reinforcement of desirable behaviours and intervention groups. In so doing I am seeking to understand perspectives and potentially offer solutions. The former is therefore research which may inform the latter.

The data obtained from this research underlines the usefulness of exploring professional practice in relation to school exclusion. Within the findings I note that by interviewing both students and staff this provides a powerful insight into what life is like for students who are excluded. Furthermore, the data illuminates the perspective of staff in relation to what they felt when excluding a student and how they feel about the process of temporary and permanent exclusion (Lamb 2005). Thus, I interview several students and teachers with a view to ascertaining their ideas with regards to the notion of exclusion. These findings will be discussed as will what action has occurred as a result of the dissemination of them. This is especially pertinent as literature is dated and more current, original work such as this, which was implemented between the years 2014 and 2017, needs to be done. Against this backdrop I now intend to explain how auto / biographical research can be implemented when seeking to critically assess the subject of school exclusion. As you read this book and its findings and recommendations – it offers insight, challenge and tentative generalisability to those following in the steps of enhancing their practice for promoting positive learning behaviour.

Chapter 2 Literature Review

2.1 Introduction to the chapter. What is school exclusion?

This chapter will explain what is meant by a school exclusion. This is important as an understanding of this is essential in forming a useful school policy about school exclusion. It will also look at the notion of biographical research into exclusion, which is the vehicle for implementing research and educational change within the school I work. Finally, I will address the issues relating to school exclusion, such as the contentions an exclusion may cause, the difficulties a headteacher may have in excluding a child, such as the system of appeal. It is also pertinent to note that there are alternatives to exclusion, which may be used prior to or instead of an exclusion. These matters are significant to this project as the data contained in chapter four discusses these issues and it is therefore important to have a background knowledge of these matters prior to the conducting and analysis of the interviews.

Exclusion can be defined as being removed from a situation, place or school, on a temporary or permanent basis. Gordon (2001:70) states: 'As those in compulsory education will know, the term exclusion refers to the expulsion or suspension of a student from school.' Arnold et al. (2009) suggests that exclusion is used to punish unacceptable behaviour towards others. This raises issues on what is deemed 'unacceptable'. Arnold et al (ibid) note that exclusion may occur if a child has severely broken the school rules and / or their presence on the school premises would hinder the rights of others to learn. Alternatively, exclusion may be used if the head teacher feels that a child's behaviour would be dangerous to themselves and others (Hants Web 2009). It is a disciplinary matter which only the head teacher or deputy or assistant head teacher, if left in charge of the school, may use to deal with inappropriate behaviour. Devon County Council (2012:1) note:

Normally, only the Headteacher can exclude a pupil. However, if the Headteacher is absent from school, the most senior teacher, who is acting on the Head's behalf, can exclude a pupil.

National guidance (Department for Education, 2011) and the current school policy see exclusion as a last resort, having exhausted other avenues, unsuccessfully to reform the individual's behaviour (City University 2011). North Yorkshire County Council (2012) state that a letter of exclusion should be sent to the parent or guardian of the pupil which outlines the incident that resulted in the exclusion, the period of exclusion and the rights the parent, or care provider has in bringing their case to the governors.

The process to which the Department for Education (2011) dictates is that there are two types of exclusion; fixed term or permanent. Fixed term exclusion is when the head teacher writes home to the pupil's parents and states that they are required to keep their child at home for a designated period of time. This would not exceed 45 days within one academic year. With an exclusion of more than one day, the school would then set work for the child, to be marked by their teacher. If a lunch time exclusion is given this constitutes a half-day exclusion, meaning that the child would be excluded from the premises for the whole lunch period. For exclusions between 5 days and 15 days, the parent has a right to ask for a meeting with the school governors, whereby they may express their views (Norbert-Obonyo et al. 2001). For an exclusion exceeding this period of time, the Pupil Disciplinary Committee (PDC) will meet with the child and parents, to discuss the pupil's record but no opportunity for appeal can be made. For a permanent exclusion, the head teacher writes to the parents / caregiver of the child and explains that they have been removed from the school roll; in this case the governors would meet to discuss and review this decision (Ruebain 1994). Brighton and Hove City Council (nd:1) state in respect of permanent exclusion: 'This means your child will not be able to return to that school again (pending the Discipline Committee hearing/independent appeal process).'

Eastman et al. (2011:126) states: 'Many schools will exhaust all possibilities before a permanent exclusion.'

The parents of a child excluded may appeal against a permanent exclusion and ask questions relating to it. If the governors agree to uphold the head teacher's decision, the parents are entitled to lodge an independent appeal against the panel. Lincolnshire County Council (2011:3) state:

> Every permanent exclusion must be considered by the school governors' Pupil Disciplinary Committee. This must happen within 15 school days of the exclusion being made. The governors can confirm the headteacher's decision to exclude your child or decide to re-instate your child at the school. If the governors uphold the exclusion, you have the right to appeal to an Independent Appeal Panel.

The appeals panel operates to decide whether or not to re-integrate the child into the school. If an appeal is not made within the prescribed time limits, a pupil is referred to a Pupil Referral Unit (PRU) in which temporary education will be offered to him or her. However, as Paton (2012) notes, the effectiveness of this system is currently being reviewed by ministers and is potentially subject to change. If, on the other hand, the head teacher's decision is overturned by the appeals panel, a date would be fixed for the child to return to school and pastoral support and agreements will be put in place to limit or prevent any further occurrences of exclusionary procedures (Great Britain Commission for Racial Equality 1997).

2.2 Biographical research into the reasons for exclusion

I will now discuss some of the reasons why school exclusions may occur. This part of the book includes the recommendations from school and national guidance of when an exclusion can be given, as well as offering data for what constituted the expulsion of the child from school. Furthermore, it suggests opportunities for which biographical work can be beneficial within this field, such as understanding the motives young people may have when they behave in a particular way.

Biographical research, as Wright et al. (2000) note, can give reasons why exclusions occurred. This can be from the perspective of the head teacher or senior management or from the child. From their research, they suggest that sometimes the leadership team made subjective and inconsistent decisions which resulted in exclusions being given. Furthermore, some of the excluded pupils were divided over how they viewed the exclusion; some felt that they were being appropriately sanctioned, whereas others were of the view that they had been unjustly dealt with. As a critical reflection biographical research may not be the only effective means of eliciting viewpoints in relation to exclusion. Wright et al. (2000) appear to adopt a paradigm which influences the way in which they conduct their work, primarily from the perspective of the pupil who has been 'unjustly' excluded. Therefore, the conclusions they draw are affected through the lens which they use to implement their work and analyse the data. Moreover, Nathan (1986) argues that the paradigm a person has and the sample size are factors which can influence the results. Furthermore, the sample size is small and may not be representational of a 'wider' and 'broader' picture. Geddes (1990) argues the selection of cases or participants by a researcher can distort the results. Have Wright et al. (ibid) selected cases which clearly illustrate their own agenda?

The reasons from the former DFES (2005:3) guidance for exclusion are:

- Exclusion is to be used as a response to a serious breach of the school rules or criminal activity
- It is not to be used for minor misconduct or slight deviance of the school policies
- It should only be used after all other reasonable attempts have been made to deal with the child in alternative ways

By way of critique, the DFES (ibid) has a fluid description of the reasons for exclusion, not specifically outlining instances whereby it may or may not be appropriate. Thus, it may be argued to be unhelpful and subjective depending upon the individual head teacher and situation. On the counter side of the argument, this allows the practitioner to exercise their professional judgement based upon the situation. The DFES (2005:4) indicated that prevalence of exclusion related to acts of disruption or violence:

Almost 30 per cent of both fixed period and permanent exclusions were due to persistent disruptive behaviour; over 20 per cent involved verbal abuse/ threatening behaviour against an adult; and 20 per cent involved physical assault against a pupil.

There are different reasons for school exclusion, which appear subjective, primarily based upon the head teacher's judgement. Appendix 2 gives some of the examples of why head teachers excluded pupils from school. It is unlikely that every head teacher will implement exclusion policies in the same way as another head teacher of a different school. Brodie (2001) suggests that from interviewing participants from different schools, the most common reasons for exclusion were for verbal or physical abuse.

Blyth and Milner (1996) are of the view that the main reasons for exclusion are disruption, verbal or physical abuse, truancy including absconding as well as criminal activity. Blyth and Milner's (ibid) sentiments concur with my own experience of teaching in a school judged to be in 'special measures' by Ofsted, whereby interviewing children revealed something of the mind of the child, who would be in trouble often for disruption or abusive behaviour. Themes that emerged are feelings relating to the difficulties the pupils had in conforming to the mainstream educational system, as well as domestic problems they were encountering. Through biographical research, reflective stories can illumine key issues in a person's experience (Webster and Mertova 2008). Narrative research may work towards answering questions such as: why is the child behaving as they are? Then again: how does the child's disruptive behaviour impact upon the teaching and learning? The Department of Health, Education, and Welfare (2011) explained that many exclusions were given for disruptive behaviour and that tackling poor persistent behaviour was a priority of the coalition government as this is, in their view, an erosion of authority and counterproductive for other class members' learning. Threads of common experiences may run throughout such biographical research revealing issues such as the impact of low level or severe disruption upon the lessons taught and how individual members of staff felt about it (Massey and Groves 2011). Furthermore, biographical research may raise questions such as do the staff feel the behaviour policy is effective in managing inappropriate behaviour?

(Hopkins 2008). Porter (2006:4) argues: '...terms such as 'misbehaviour' or 'inappropriate behaviour' do not specify to whom these acts are inappropriate.' This is a challenging point as it may cause staff to reflect upon their notion of 'appropriate' or 'inappropriate.' A further question could be raised: do staff feel that matters relating to exclusion are deal with appropriately? Cooper (2002) states that attitudes such as discontentment and lack of senior management support may emerge from interviews. On the counter side, some may suggest that they feel adequately supported and are content that the discipline policy is effective in curtailing unacceptable behaviour (Pritchard 2009).

2.3 School Exclusion- what are the problems? Biographical research into the problematic nature of an exclusion

I will now discuss the potential pitfalls from a biographical perspective associated with excluding a child from school. These include how some head teachers may be disempowered as they face their decision being undermined by a governing body. Furthermore, this section discusses how the sanction may be viewed at home and the implications of this upon domestic life. The dilemmas school leaders face when seeking to exclude a child with SEN are also outlined as complex and debatable. Narrative enquiry may reveal how individuals manage in different situations, such as how family life may be adversely affected through an exclusion. Alternatively, biographical research may help to understand how a head teacher may feel if their decision was countermanded.

2.3.1 Head teacher being overruled

In some situations, a head teacher desiring to promote inclusion may feel it necessary to exclude a child (The Learning Trust 2004). However, Lipsett (2008) reports if a headteacher's decision is undermined by the governors or an appeals panel to integrate the child back into school, the head teacher may feel undermined. Gove (2007) called for the head teacher's decision to be backed up without the threat that their decision may be overruled. Successful appeals formed 21 percent of those lodged in 2005 and 24 percent in 2006, an increase from the previous year favouring the parent and pupil. Moreover, Gove (2007:34) argued, discipline is crucial, 'head teachers should be able to exclude disruptive pupils without being second guessed (by appeals panels).' On the contrary, Haydn and Martin (2011:34) state that recent government rhetoric has focused upon discipline and exclusion, which follow a criminalisation policy, which in Haydn and Martin's view is unhelpful:

The talk is certainly tough. While Conservative policy includes more traditional school discipline measures such as, detentions, talk of searches, confiscation and removal of rights continues the criminalising discourse. We believe more progressive education policy would be to decriminalise school safety and discipline issues.

Against this background, biographical work could offer a voice for the head teacher to be heard. Data could reveal how disempowered individuals may feel by the appeals process. For example, head teachers may disclose that they felt that their decision had been undermined and by having the child back in school they had lost the respect of the child and their family (Kitching 2001). Subsequently, if the child (after re- integration) continued to behave inappropriately, the head teacher's options would be limited. The field of literature for this type of research is currently minimal, with the exception of articles and reports which comment upon the possibility of the exclusion process disempowering school leaders (Dyke 2011, Garner 2009, Gove 2007). Therefore, by interviewing the headteacher I can ask him how he feels about the exclusion process, seeking to contribute to the body of research.

The alternative argument is that the head teacher is accountable for their decisions and an appeals panel provides this (IPSEA 2001). It may also help a child to be reintegrated into the school, if their appeal is successful. Harris and Eden (2000:6) argue: 'The appeal system is important because permanent exclusion from a school is a serious matter.' This, they state, is imperative as the child may have their education disrupted by being permanently expelled, having a detrimental impact upon their development.

An opportunity for biographical work may occur here, as a tribunal may offer the child or parent/s the opportunity to discuss, at a greater length than normal, their life story (McAra 2004). This can offer insights from biographical perspectives into why the child has decided to behave in a certain way. It is pertinent to note that the literature in this matter is sparse. Therefore, this work may be considered as timely and useful. Research within this field may illume issues which the head teacher may be unaware of such as specific problems at home or difficulties incurred at school. Wright et al. (2005:28) conduct biographical research and note Miranda's response to her exclusion: 'when I was at home [after exclusion] and didn't have anything to do, I was just thinking right I'm not going to get any GCSEs and can't get a job...' McLeod (2008) suggests that by listening to individuals, a picture of their life is painted before you and reasons for their conduct become clearer. Furthermore, Harris and Eden (2000) are of the view that due to the serious nature of exclusion, an appeal gives them opportunities for both sides to be represented. However, they do admit that whilst an appeal is implemented, the child's presence back at school may disrupt the learning of the other students. Thus, both sides of the argument are in view in Harris and Eden's sentiments. Garner (2009) argues that if young people have the right to appeal they may use this as a license to misbehave or remind staff that even if they are excluded the appeal may work in their favour, thus, undermining the process. Biographical work could also be extended to hearing the voices of the others in the class. How do they feel about having a child who has been excluded being back in school potentially causing disruption? Such research may have mixed outcomes; some focusing upon the child's presence as a positive, others suggesting that their behaviour was detrimental to their education and that of the class in general.

Another perspective is offered by Wright et al. (2000:15) who suggest: 'Indeed exclusion may say more about the needs of the school than it does about the pupil being excluded.' This viewpoint emphasises that schools should seek to avoid excluding a child through implementing appropriate provision. Thus, an exclusion, in Wright et al's. (ibid) view highlights a deficit in the schools' resources. In this area, biographical research could provide powerful insights into the opinions of staff and pupils relating to the current provision for more challenging behaviour. Macrae and Maguire (2003) suggest that school exclusion should be challenged and alternatives are far more suitable. The counter side to this argument is that the school may choose to exclude to benefit those who are not breaking the rules and have to observe others flouting the rules without serious consequence (Osler et al. 2000). Moreover, biographies of those who hold to this viewpoint may offer an interviewee, such as the headteacher, opportunities to explain their policies and standards (Martin et al. 1999).

2.3.2 Biographical insights into the contention school exclusion may cause for parents, pupils and staff

Biographical research can highlight potential problems that that exclusion may cause. For example, a child or family may view the sanction of exclusion as insignificant. Furthermore, there are implications of exclusion which may impact upon the family life. I will also take up the point Blyth and Milner (1996) make that there has been and is a concern about the welfare and education of those who are excluded. Kane (2011:137) argues that exclusion can be detrimental in obtaining adequate educational experiences and qualifications. She further states that the system needs to be adaptable to the needs of individuals and the wider community:

Repeated experience of school exclusion was seen to undermine and sometimes destroy pupils' participation in schooling and to deny them benefits accruing from education and formal credentials. The manner in which exclusions are reduced is such that pupils are usually left still on the margins of schooling, attached but not involved. School approaches to tackling exclusion would require greater flexibility of provision for all pupils and much stronger attempts to engage pupils, families and communities in articulating the purposes of schooling and in designing curricular paths related to those purposes.

The sanction of exclusion may also be seen as an inconvenience and needs to be considered carefully in terms of equal rights and opportunities (Parkes 2012). In addition to this, some families may not be able to supervise their children due to other commitments, subsequently, allowing their children to play at home or roam the streets. Thus, as Evans (2010) argues, in such cases exclusion may be inappropriate as a sanction. Biographical research, seeking to ascertain the opinions of parents relating to the exclusion process, could make insightful reading relating to their perception of whether exclusion is the most effective means of discipline for their child. Cohen et al. (1994) assert that an exclusion may cause parental inconvenience at not being able to go to work as they have to supervise their child. For example, from my own practice of teaching a child six years ago, who, despite infringing the rules to a high degree, was not excluded. This was because the acting head teacher felt that the parent would not punish their child but allow them to watch television and to go to the town to play and socialise. Thus, in the head teacher's view, the sanction was being undermined. Instead of being a punishment it would be a reward; a day or more off school. It would be interesting to use biographical research to gain differing perspectives upon this issue.

There are also implications of exclusion upon the child who is excluded and their family. Berridge et al. (2001) noted from qualitative research that parents said that during the exclusion process, they felt isolated and uninformed. In one case, whereby a permanent exclusion was upheld, the Education Authority took an excessively long time to make adequate educational provision for their child, causing anxiety and strained domestic relationships. These sentiments concur with Wright et al. (2005) who suggest that exclusion can have a detrimental impact upon those involved in the process. Moreover, they highlight that some parents and pupils were left in a state of 'educational limbo' (p. 32) due to inadequate provision. Wright et al.'s work appears flawed in the research as the research objective appears to begin with the premise of seeking to unearth problems with exclusion, rather than letting the data 'speak for itself.' Biographical research can uncover issues such as perceived inequalities in the system and elicit the feelings of both parents and pupils who are involved in the exclusionary process.

Briggs (2011:14) who conducted biographical research into the feelings of those who had been excluded notes:

> The consequences of permanent exclusion often result in lack of education, heightened family stress, fewer opportunities to acquire skills and qualifications required in the labour market and social exclusion.

Table 2.3.2.1   Some of the possible implications that expulsion may have (Munn et al. 2000: 12).

Problem caused:	Effect of this problem:
Irritation with the excluded child.	Getting on the parent / carers nerves, in the way.
Inconvenienced.	Felt they cannot do the housework or go to work whilst their child is at home.
Stress caused.	Angry, puts them in a negative frame of mind.
Family arguments.	Reprimanded or sanctioned at home. Causes problems with parent /s.
Comparisons made.	Child is compared to their siblings, producing negativity and resentment / reluctance.

Munn et al. (2000:2) interviewed children in Scotland about their experiences of school exclusion. It is clear that some of those who were interviewed were uncertain as to what the future of their education would be. Others had emotional responses varying from anger to upset. Biographical research may illuminate issues that are indicative of the viewpoints expressed by those who have been excluded (Berridge et al. 2001). However, Munn et al's research is geographically focussed upon Scotland and may not be reflective of a wider 'picture.'

Nonetheless, some of the feelings interviewees experienced are recorded below:

- Rejected / unwanted.

- Angry and feeling they wanted revenge.

- Hard done by, the not fair factor.

- Worried about their parents' reactions.

- Upset / scared and shocked.

The children stated that their explanation of the events had not been heard or duly considered. Narrative inquiry would, in my opinion, be both interesting and useful. In the context of its usefulness, the school may benefit from hearing the pupil's perception of for example an injustice. Rogers (2006) uses this type of work and records that pupils had stated that teachers would often act inconsistently when dealing with inappropriate behaviour. This would give the wrong messages out and cause a sense of confusion. The interviewees from Roger's work commented that a lot depended upon the teacher's mood, the child who had committed the offence, their general feelings at the time of the breaking of the rule and a range of factors surrounding the practitioner's disposition towards the offender. Bracher (2003) infers that biographical work could give such children the opportunity to 'sound off,' and this may help the child to break an iterative pattern of inappropriate behaviour. However, there is an insufficient amount of literature at present to make a definite case for this argument.

From personal experience, the impact of exclusion can lead a child to experience a range of problems. Dix (2010:126) argues, 'A student who is repeatedly excluded is likely to be in a cycle of negative behaviour.' The cyclical nature of the problem being; inappropriate behaviour exhibited, excluded, low self – esteem, negative attitude / anger towards the school. Biographical work could elicit these types of feelings, revealing children who are potentially unhappy and are currently in a pattern of poor behaviour; subsequently their expectations and others are decreased (Brodie 2001).

A further issue relating to problems of school exclusion from a biographical analysis point of view is the difficulties exclusion places upon domestic life (Munn et al., ibid). Over ten years ago I taught a child who was given a fixed-term exclusion and then re-appeared the next day as the single mother claimed that she had to go to work and had no means of supervising her son. The exclusion was seen by the mother in a negative light, one of the reasons being that she had to manage her child's challenging behaviour at home and was subsequently prevented from work. The child also expressed great anger towards the school and particularly the headteacher, which led to an extension of the fixed-term exclusion being given. Moreover, exclusion is not a simplistic matter but has implications beyond the initial expulsion. On the opposite side of the argument, Harris and Eden (2000) are of the view that sometimes a permanent exclusion is helpful to ensure that the child's needs are met. The child in the anecdote above ended up being permanently excluded and eventually obtaining a place in a special school which was, in his case, a more suitable form of provision. However, this was not a one-dimensional process and I would argue not a universal panacea, due to the distress and problems it created. From a previous informal interview with the parent cited in the above anecdote, I learnt that she had difficulties in adequately managing effective discipline of her child within the home. Therefore, she was displeased with having to have her child at home during school hours.

Cullingford (1999) is of the view that sometimes children who are excluded are dissatisfied, feeling as though they have 'failed' (p. 112) in the system. They may therefore seek to fight the system and the teachers within it. Cullingford (ibid) further argues that several pupils felt as though they were not welcome at school because of who they were and how they behaved. Biographical research into pupil dissatisfaction is associated with Kinder and Wilkin (1998), who identified how pupils felt about school. Some of the findings were that pupils felt that assistance and sustained support was not readily available, clear learning intentions in core subjects were not apparent, poor relationships between staff and students existed, as well as feeling that they were not coping with the curriculum's requirements. There are significant potential research opportunities here, such as interviewing school-aged children and seeking to elicit their viewpoint (Peddler and McIntyre 2007). A number of pertinent issues were raised such as their lack of interest towards school work, feeling that they were estranged from adult help and that their needs were inadequately met. I discuss biographical research into school exclusion of those with special needs in Appendix 3.

2.4 Exclusions – are there alternatives? Biographical research into other options

This subsection addresses the alternatives that head teachers may consider before an exclusion is made. It may also act as a way of avoiding the expulsion of a pupil. It includes the whole school policy being revised and adapted to a becoming a more inclusive culture (Atkinson 1997). This in turn has associated issues such as: what does inclusion mean? Clemson and Clemson (1990) infer that biographical research can open up opportunities to allow participants to share their opinions relating to the alternatives to exclusion.

Cooper (2002) argues that there are alternatives to exclusion which should be considered before making a fixed term or permanent exclusion. Some of these alternatives are:

- Effective sanctioning.
- Positive reinforcement, i.e. praise.
- Sending them home (to calm down and reflect upon their behaviour)
- Internal exclusion / isolation.
- Attendance, which is part time or adjustments, made to their time tables.
- Sending them to different members of staff or to a certain quiet area or unit.

Blair (2001) states that alternatives to exclusion may be addressed as a whole school approach, which seeks to actively promote positive behaviour and inclusion. (Inclusion is a value laden term which Appendix 4 explores in greater detail). Hallam and Castle (2001) argue that the use of multi-disciplinary behaviour support and in – school centres have proved to reduce exclusion rates. Moreover, Bennathan and Boxall (2008) suggest that nurture groups are an example of an effective form of intervention in preventing inappropriate behaviour and encouraging a calm and happy ethos. These sentiments are echoed by Ofsted (2009:6):

> The nine schools that had nurture groups found these were essential provision in supporting young children who were most in need and who displayed complex and compound behaviours.

However, a critique of Ofsted's report is that it does not specify what 'complex and compound' means. This would help to clarify the usefulness of nurture group sessions in the light of a clearer understanding of these notions.

Further to this point, Pryce- Jones and Lutterbie (2010) identify that a strong correlation between happiness and motivation to work exists. They state from empirical research that the 'highest happiness group' had the largest number of people who remained on task for the longest amount of time (80%). This applied to the classroom context, has ramifications upon pupil – teacher relationships and how happy both are. However, I would postulate that the control of variables appears superficial in this experiment, the conclusions seem generic and insufficient. Therefore, the research should be judged within the light of the publishing of its work. However, it may be argued that biographical work has potential to shed light upon the feelings of the individuals within the exclusion process and such data may have connections to the levels of happiness a person is showing which in turn may manifest itself in an improvement or decline of behavioural standards (Oakes 2012). However, Carver and Scheier (2008:93) state: '...people may often be unaware of the motives behind problem behaviours.'

Davies (1999) argues that positive reinforcement is a good way to promote the desirable and gain a greater understanding of any issue associated with behaviour. She noted from her studies that loss of breaks and lunches were an effective sanction. However, they had a wearing down effect upon staff that would have to conduct them in their own time. A weakness of Davies (ibid) work is that it does not specifically highlight how she will ascertain positive behaviour or delve beneath the surface and look at inappropriate behaviour in more depth. Briggs (2011:89) argues that 'more motivational approaches' are required and the use of exclusion for serious matters, rather than 'minor misdemeanours.' This research has been carried out through biographical studies, asking the pupils their motives and intentions in breaking rules and whether or not they see alternatives to exclusion as an effective sanction. The sample used in this study was based upon one geographical region (London), and it may be argued not to be generalisable beyond the geographical parameters of the study. Ruddock and McIntyre (2007) argue that by listening to an individual they may choose to explain their reasons for a type of behaviour as well as share their problems. A potential drawback of this work (Ruddock and McIntyre, (ibid)) is that it is idealistic and assumes all children want to talk about their behaviour, which may not necessarily be the case. In addition, it does not present an objective case for the use of exclusion, such as the alternatives to exclusion which may be negotiated and discussed with the individuals concerned.

Chapter 3   Research Methods and Methodology

This chapter focuses upon the research methods employed and the methodologies underlying them.   This project has focused upon using biographical research to find out about school exclusion as a process of exploring and evaluating professional practice. In so doing I shall critique the arguments and interpretations of different authors, suggesting where their arguments may be flawed and where 'gaps' are within the published literature.

3.1   Investigating school exclusion

Narrative research focuses upon human experience within a life story (Webster and Mertova 2007). Stanley (1992:178) notes, 'writing biographic processes makes visible the existence of something usually invisible and effectively denied.'   These sentiments of Stanley (ibid) suggest that biographical research can allow an individual to express their viewpoint, which they may not have had the chance to do so before. Stanley (ibid) uses powerful phases such as 'invisible' and 'denied' to convey meaning and the power associated with this research method. However, to suggest something is 'invisible' or 'denied' is a powerful and emotive image.   Ethington (2004:85) uses the term 'partially' to describe the impact of her work: 'There are some voices that have been only partially heard.'   Perhaps Erben (2000:383) highlights the case for narrative with greater clarity and objectivity: 'Lives are lived through time but made intelligible through narrative'? Roberts (2002:82) states: 'Auto/biography has placed considerable emphasis on the place of time within biographical research...' The research I shall conduct is a fragment of a life within the realm of time, it is therefore important to contextualise and foreground any biography and the views expressed within them (Gillies 2009).

Cooper (2002) suggests that biographies can help a person gain an understanding of the many and varied issues associated with school exclusion.

To take this point to a logical conclusion, biographical work can draw upon the views of the excluded as well as the head teacher and staff involved in the exclusion process. Punch (2009:191) argues: 'Narratives and stories are also valuable in studying lives and lived experience, as is often demonstrated in studies concerned with empowerment.' To synthesise this argument, Punch (ibid) is of the opinion that narrative research is of benefit in eliciting views and empowering others to share their experiences. However, Punch (ibid) does not cite a specific study or refer to any outcomes as a result of research. On the contrary, Bornat and Tetley (2010) argue that oral story telling may not be empowering for some participants. Furthermore, the paradigm Punch (ibid) adopts would impact upon the way in which he views the research process and the methodologies selected. May and Perry (2011: 105) state: 'We are all situated within the socio- cultural milieu of which we are a part.' These thoughts underpin the positioning of the researcher to the research. Blake (2003) stresses this point; the epistemological view of the researcher may influence the thoughts, actions and decisions made. As a result, Punch's sentiments appear subjective and unsubstantiated. As a counter argument Wilson (2010) argues that the idea of subjectivity should be re-thought. She suggests that the subject cannot be detached from the object.

Wilson (2010:257) summarises:

> So the very thing that supposedly gets in the way – your subjective humanness and its inevitable preconceptions, lenses and biases- is also the very thing that allows you to reach across the distance and make meaning out of your object.

Denzin (2001:3) succinctly describes the relationship between the researcher and the research: 'The qualitative researcher is not an objective, politically neutral observer who stands outside and above the study of the social world.' Denzin (ibid) further explains that is both locally and historically situated within the research process. Thus, when asking an interviewee about their experiences the work cannot, within Denzin's view, be detached from the values it carries. Furthermore, Gray (2002) is of the view that asking individuals about their experiences may provide powerful insights into the thinking of an individual, whether that is of the practitioner or the pupil, which helps to shape the practitioners ideas in relation to possible revision of school exclusion policies. To critique this idea, some children are shy and / or unwilling to share their ideas (Altrichter et al. 2009). Therefore, this type of method may be ineffective in eliciting the viewpoint of these children or staff.

On the other hand, Atkinson (1998:7) holds the opinion: 'Telling our story enables us to be heard, recognised, and acknowledged by others. Story makes the implicit explicit, the hidden seen, the unformed formed, and the confusing clear.' This is a pertinent point as the process of exclusion can be bewildering for staff, governors, students and parents. However, if critically synthesising the sentiments of Atkinson (ibid), children and staff may tell confusing, ambiguous stories which may not add clarity to the data collected (Drever 2006). Therefore, although telling a story can be useful, it may not have the attached benefits of the clarity and empowerment Atkinson (ibid) suggests.

3.2 Methodological issues associated with biographical research

I will now address the methodological points associated with this type of work. I shall design, apply and critically evaluate methods of data collection and analysis.

There are specific benefits and limitations of the interview. I shall begin with these limitations and then draw upon how the strengths of this type of methodological approach outweigh the potential disadvantages of its usage within my field of study.

First, when interviewing students, I wanted the interviewee to reveal their thoughts and ideas in relation to school exclusion. This is difficult for some children as they may find it hard to articulate their point of view (Hopkins 2008). Mertens and McLaughlin (2004) argue that interviews with children and those with special needs can be problematic, as they may not understand the questions asked or may feel shy in answering them. I was therefore sensitive in my approach, seeking to develop a positive relationship with participants and as far as possible asked questions in a clear way. Holmes (1998:23) takes the following approach:

I neither conduct structured interviews with the children nor intentionally take them out of their classroom for the purpose of interviewing them. The latter situation is anxiety producing for them, and the children equate being separated from their class mates with the notion that they have misbehaved in some way. I find that informal or unstructured interviewing (during free play in the classroom, on the playground, on the bus and so forth) works most effectively, and I have integrated asking children to draw for me while I am talking with them.

Holmes (ibid) takes an interesting approach when interviewing, by encouraging children to speak with him, whilst drawing, to relieve tension and do something they enjoy doing. However, it may be unhelpful to interview on the playground, whilst the child is trying to play or during their golden time (unstructured free-flow play in class) as the child may just wish to play or answer quickly or as they think Holmes might have wanted to hear. Furthermore, it appears unethical, unless permission had been granted by the child and carer that Holmes did as he did, as a child may not be aware that what they were saying, informally, would form the basis of Holmes research. Therefore, within my research I sought to ask questions through interviews, which took place away from others and asked the interviewee whether they would be prepared to speak with me. Within this I sought to make clear what their participation in the research meant. Noffke and Somekh (2009:92) ask: 'Who is included in the research? Was consideration given to including everyone with an involvement?' Noffke and Somekh (ibid) continue to identify the means to which this should be done, carefully asking for volunteers and explaining the ramifications of their involvement. However, Corbin and Strauss (2008) note that one particular drawback of an interview is that the interviewee, after agreeing to participate, may have very little to share and either disclose little or remain silent for much of the interview. In this situation I should direct different questions and be sensitive to the mood and flow of the interview. It should be noted that the interviewee cannot be coerced into speaking, however, the way in which the interview is conducted can help to prevent periods of silence (Johns 2009).

Another key point is made by Clough and Barton (1998) who explain that sometimes both interviewees and interviewers respond to or ask questions with anecdotes and opinions in a value - carrying way. Although no research is value-free, I sought to critically reflect upon the formation of questions asked, to ensure that my viewpoint did not reflect the way in which I asked a question. Becker (1967:239) argues that it is an impossibility to conduct research which is 'uncontaminated by personal and political sympathies.' Moreover, as Riessman (2008) states, the way in which an interviewer listens and questions shapes the interviewees' responses. If dialogues are to be honest reflections of personal experience, a researcher should seek to avoid emotive questions, responses and reactions. I therefore tried to consciously ensure that I did not ask 'loaded questions', reflecting personal opinions. This is important as my agenda and own ideas could be imposed upon those that I interviewed, creating invalid data (Herr and Anderson 2005).

Furthermore, there are other disadvantages of interviewing within biographical methods; including the issue of power relationships that may exist between myself and the interviewee. By this I refer to the potential perceived differences of power and authority that may exist between an adult (researcher) and the student (participant). This could potentially inhibit interaction as a respondent may feel uncomfortable in the presence of me as the researcher. In so doing as Drever (2006) argues that the respondent may answer according to that which they perceive the interviewer desires to hear. Thus, as a result of this, inaccurate data could be generated. To critique Drever's ideas it may be noted that the interviewee may not answer according to how they feel the interviewer would like to hear. Cooper (2002) suggests that interviewing can allow a person liberty to freely express their ideas, even if these ideas are controversial or emotive. When I conducted the interview I sought to appear in a non- threatening manner, presenting myself as an 'equal' to try to promote unhindered interaction, which as far as possible was based upon the truth. McLeod (2009) argues that the practitioner should 'address power issues' (p.118) and not impose a predetermined agenda upon an interviewee. I have sought to overcome or limit the impact of power relationships by explaining to potential participants that their contribution was entirely voluntarily and that if they chose not to participate they were within their rights to do so. Furthermore, I sought to make clear that there would be no reprisals and no potential detriment would occur if they did not wish to participate. This was important as I did not wish people to participate unwillingly just to please me or prevent what they may have seen as a sanction or my displeasure. Thus, from the outset of this project I explained that the students did not have to participate and that any interview was done on a voluntary basis, in which they could withdraw or terminate it at any point.

Denscombe (2006) suggests that the interview is based upon what a person claims to be like or to have done, when the reality may be quite different. Denscombe (2006:190) argues in relation to this point: 'In particular, interviewee statements can be affected by the identity of the researcher.' A way to limit the effect of this is to reflexively ask: how do I present myself? (Cohen et al. 2007). Within this self – examination, the interviewee may consider putting the student at ease and asking for an honest open dialogue, whereby the interviewer makes it clear that they are not standing in judgement. I sought to adopt this approach, which seemed to reap rewards in the students and staff sharing their ideas freely. Flick et al. (2008) argue that the interviewer need not explain their position in relation to a particular issue, in this case exclusion, rather seek to maintain a neutral stance. Thus, a key component of generating reliable data is in seeking to limit the impact of imposing values and minimise the effects created through a power relationship.

Interviews rely upon individuals sharing aspects of a life story. Denzin (1989:74) argues: 'A story is always an interpretive account; but, of course, all interpretations are biased.' Sikes and Gale (2006:3) also state: 'No story of a life or an aspect of a life, can be anything other than an interpretation, a re-presentation.' Within the implementation of this research methodology, I needed to be aware that students who are excluded will only be giving a one-sided account of their experiences. To give an example of this from a different discipline, Wheelock (2007) when interviewing about nutrition and achievement, noted that some participants appeared more willing than others and were happy to share their ideas, however when they did so some of the sentiments appear highly subjective. Her research claims to have led her to the conclusion that there was a correlation between healthy eating in schools and behaviour. Although it is not my purpose to synthesise this argument, it is pertinent to note that behaviour and nutrition may be linked. However, I would question the validity and reliability of Wheelock's work, as the publishing house identifies her as the source of publishing. Therefore, she has published her own work, which has not been subject to peer review. When interviewing staff, they too will inevitably bring their own slant upon the situation, thus, the analysis of such data needs to be carefully considered and specific claims evaluated in the light of this (Gilgun 2010). It is significant to critically evaluate their ideas whilst reflecting on the methods used to investigate exclusion policies. Further to this, it is pertinent to critique and use this data to inform the development and impact of educational practice. Moreover, Dhunpath and Samuel (2009:93) argue: 'The notion of trust in narrative knowledge creation is of great significance to me.' These ideas by Dhunpath and Samuel (ibid) are important in the respect of the notion of trust, as defined by Derlega et al. (2005:490) 'Trust is one of the most important factors in the development of relationships.' However, the creation of knowledge is upon tentative grounds, as this assumes a foundation to knowledge and raises epistemological questions about what is knowledge? Piper and Stronach (2004:35, emphasis added) note: '...what constitutes warranted knowledge claims (knowing or epistemology) [are within some aspects of research] at centre stage.' For the benefit of this work I shall raise this issue and suggest that an entire study in its own right would be needed to address this (Popper and Eccles 1977, Popper 1992, Sosa et al. 2011). Dhunpath and Samuel (ibid) use terms such as 'knowledge creation', which are loaded with value and significance (Girard et al. 2011, Baehr 2011).

I will now address the specific benefits of using interviews in biographical work. First, the interview allows for more depth and breadth of study. According to Bryman (2008) rich accounts of thick description can be generated. However, there are other theorists, such as Suter (2012) that disagree with this and highlight the benefits of other methods, such as the volume of data that can be generated from questionnaires. By contrast, Yin (2010) expresses the specific benefit that biographical work can bring. He notes that the case study research opens opportunities to explore issues which reflect the interviewee's ideas and beliefs about the world and their current situation. However, these sentiments in isolation appear to lack academic rigour as relationships need to be formed prior to disclosures being made (Dhunpath and Samuel 2009).

Within a relationship of trust and respect, mutually understood and agreed, sensitive issues can be explored and personal accounts can be shared (Elton- Chalcraft et al. 2008). Dawson (2009:28) states: 'Researchers have to be able to establish rapport with the participant – they have to be trusted if someone is to reveal intimate life information.' The beneficial implications of developing such a relationship are that the participant may feel much more able to share information they would not otherwise have done. However, there is no guarantee that this will occur (Robson 2010).

A further benefit of interviewing is that I can probe the interviewee for more information, if required. Greene and Hogan (2009) allege that this is a unique aspect of this type of research method and can have notable benefits in generating a holistic overview of an issue. These sentiments highlight that interviews can also help develop a pertinent issue which derive from a specific response as part of the interview. Breen (2009:19) is of the view that probing can be implemented through statements such as: '...do you remember anything more about...?' Within my interview technique I benefited from 'probing' further into issues that staff and students raised. Thus, it also helped clarify an ambiguous point and expound upon a particular matter. Radnor (2002:62) states: 'Because the interview is semi- structured, unexpected areas of interest might arise and lead to other questions worth asking.' Having made the case for these benefits, I need to be aware of when to probe as not to interrupt the dialogue or to develop questions which go off on a tangent (Bell 2005). However, some theorists would disagree with Greene and Hogan (ibid) and argue that other methods can allow a researcher opportunities for asking further questions. For example, Bulmer et al. (2004) suggest that questionnaires and interviews used in conjunction with one another can provide 'probing' opportunities.

In addition to the positive aspects raised when conducting interviews, it is arguably evident that through the use of this research method, participants involved in the research have been given opportunities to share, at length, their life experiences, specifically related to school exclusion. Mc Niff and Whitehead (2006) argue that practitioners should be heard and biographical work, including interviews is one way to do this. They suggest: 'You need to tell your story of what you are doing to sustain it and develop it even further' (p. 190). This type of research helps a person to reflectively focus upon what they are doing and why they are doing it. For instance, a professional may consider how the exclusion policy is implemented, whereas the person who has been excluded may critically assess the impact of the policy upon them (Foddy 1993). However, as Nathan (1986) argues, this may be difficult to do for some people as they lack the ability to express their ideas or be detached from emotive responses.

Cullingford (2008:27) suggests that qualitative research of this nature is far richer than quantitative:

> They provide better than any empirical approach, insights into the significant events and relationships in their lives and demonstrate the richness of data that can be provided by this method.

The sentiments by Cullingford (ibid) are generic and do not specifically take into account the substantial amounts of data that can be obtained by other methods, thus producing a biased view of this method. Through interviewing different people, multifaceted perspectives can be offered upon the issues affecting them relating to school exclusion. This project also benefited from triangulation of interviewees. Moreover, I interviewed students, teachers and the headteacher. Triangulation can be defined as the use of three different perspectives, each offering an individual response and a unique insight into the research. Basit (2010:67) argues:

Triangulation is a strategy that is used to establish concurrent validity in research by looking at the same issue from different perspectives.

A potential limitation of this research is that it did not use triangulation in the research methods, rather within those asked to participate in the interviews. However, biographical work lends itself to interviews rather than for example observation or questionnaires / surveys.

3.3 Ethical issues

Ethics forms an integral part of the research process, Mac Gilchrist and Savage (1995:43) draw upon their own research noting: 'Ethical factors were an important part of our considerations.' Fraenkel and Wallen (2008) describe ethics as that which is right and wrong. These sentiments by Fraenkel and Wallen (ibid) explain that if researchers embark upon a line of enquiry they should ask themselves whether or not it is 'right' (p. 53) to implement their research project. Singer and Biegel (2010) use the terms ethics and morality interchangeably as ways to describe what is right. However, Punch (2009) does not use the notion of ethics in terms of 'right' or 'wrong' rather he uses the term 'integrity' to describe the practice educational research should adopt.

First, the interview should be conducted with integrity. Clandinin and Connelly (2000) make the case for ethics being a key component of good practice within biographical research. Within this research, I have asked through informed consent, for participants (Elton Chalcraft et al. 2008). Informed consent refers to all potential participants being given specific information relating to the research and ensuring they understand the implications of their participation. If consent is by proxy, in relation to children, parental permission should be gained (Silverman 2009). Greene and Hogan (2009:65) suggest that ethical considerations include four key principles:

- Involvement of children in research
- Consent and choice
- Possible harm or distress
- Privacy and confidentiality

The considerations by Greene and Hogan (ibid) give a 'broad brush' approach to ethical issues. There are other factors such as identifying how the data may impact upon those who read it that are not mentioned. For example, what if a person recognises themselves within a description? Dawson (2009) notes that anonymity and careful consideration to how the data is written up is important. However, to what extent does this protect this occurring? I shall now explore some of the points relating to ethical considerations.

In my research permission from staff, parents and students has been sought by means of written confirmation. This involved negotiating with 'gate keepers' and asking for volunteers, who were willing to participate in the research. Cohen et al. (2011:79) state: 'Researchers, therefore, have an ethical obligation to seek informed consent of gatekeepers.' These sentiments have ramifications upon my practice and Cohen et al. (ibid) succinctly summarise them. In addition, Campbell and Groundwater- Smith (2007:85) make a valuable point: 'The term 'participant' has been used...rather than the other often used term 'subject.' This, they argue, is because 'participant' suggests a willing acceptance to be a part of the research and not someone who has been coerced into it. Within this research I use the terms 'participant' or 'interviewee' as they imply agreed consent.

I have also ensured the anonymity of the students used within the research. This involved using pseudonyms or initials to ensure the non-attribution of sources. I have ensured that everyone else referred to in this work is represented truthfully and wherever possible I have asked them to verify what I have written as true statements of them and their actions. Where this was not possible, for example, I no longer know where they live, or they have moved to another school I asked others who knew them to verify my account of them. Robson (2002) describes ethical research as that which 'protects' (p. 67) the participant from any reprisals through their decision to participate and equally not to be a part of the research. If participants are given pseudonyms, there is less likely to be any reprisal for comments made during an interview as the source cannot be traced. However, if a student or member of staff knows that the data will not be sensitively handled and managed, there may be a reluctance to participate or to expose sensitive information relating to school exclusion (Kay and Hinds 2007). Thus, this includes asking for the participants' permission at all stages of the research, including the analysis of data and the dissemination. Within this permission I explained the purpose of the research and what the results were going to be used for and how they would be presented. Additionally, within the analysis of responses there is the requirement to ensure the accuracy of the interpretation of data. One potential issue I found with seeking anonymity of the students involved in the research was that although the number of exclusions were higher than other schools within the catchment area, the same children were often excluded on many occasions. Therefore, identifying who the child was, if mentioned within my research findings, could be relatively straightforward to someone with internal knowledge. I therefore had to explain to all participants that although pseudonyms would be used people who read this research may be able to identify who they were. Thus, this presented an ethical dilemma in the collection of data. In the light of this all participants agreed that they were comfortable with the possibility of this occurring.

3.4   Validity and Reliability of the research methods

The two key terms validity and reliability**Error! Bookmark not defined.** are to be explored in this next sub section. Lincoln and Guba (1985:218) state: 'The conventional criteria for trustworthiness are internal validity, external validity, reliability and objectivity.' This work will seek to define them and address their role within this project. I intend to highlight specific ways in which I have addressed these principles within this book.

Furthermore, I will address how the research has sought to uphold them and enhance them within the specific aims and objectives of the research.

3.4.1   Validity

Validity is concerned with being confident that the tool used to obtain data is measuring what it claims to measure (Coolican 2009). It should be noted that the tool is also subjective as Grbich (2009:22) states:

> Subjective approaches are defined as those where there is a focus on you I and on what takes place within your own mind, recognising that this is limited by your own biases and judgements.

Validity, for the benefit of this work can be divided into two main heads; internal and external.

Internal validity refers to the changes observed in the dependent variable in relation to the independent variable. If the extraneous variables are controlled, the results are arguably internally valid (Mertens 2005). The instrumentation can pose problems with the internal validity of the project. This may occur when there are changes made to the instruments used to make the measurements (Thorsdottir 2005). Therefore, it could be argued that if the tool is altered during the research, it cannot be known whether or not the change was due to the independent variable or the alterations to the approach adopted in which the dependent variable was measured (Brinberg and Kidder 1982). For the purpose of this project I am consistently using interviews throughout the data collection stage, which does not rely in the same way upon quantitative controls.

External validity refers to the extent to which one research project and its data can be applied to another situation (Walker 2011) or the generalisability (Bryman 2015). Sapsford and Jupp (2008) argue that a way to assess validity is to ascertain whether or not the study can be replicated. The external validity in this case is the generalisability of data obtained from the participants compared to the wider population. This is specifically important to this research project as the findings can be used to make generalisations about the nature, feature and characteristics of school exclusion, without going beyond what the data suggests but at the same time being confident in the findings obtained from this work. Silverman (2008) is of the view that I should feel confident about the sample they have chosen for the project is a representation of the defined criteria. This can then be used to make generalisations about the wider population. The generalisability asks whether the information of this study can be used more universally beyond the single case study (Cohen et al. 2017). This may involve making comparisons between the results obtained and other scenarios (Kirk and Miller 1986). I would postulate that the data can be used cautiously to inform practice for other schools but would not seek to paint a picture of national trends or issue a blanket approach to forming school policies.

3.4.2   Reliability

The term reliability refers to something reliable; being dependable or trustworthy. Moreover, Hardwick and Worsley (2011:116) suggest that:

> Reliability refers to you carrying out your research well enough so that anyone following in its footsteps would be likely to find the same outcome as you did.

In data collection and analysis, a tool used to gather data should produce the same results when re-tested on the same people at another time. Oppenheim (1992) argues that reliability is the extent to which the work can be repeated, producing similar results. Within this project the use of every biographical account will be unique and therefore the type of data generated may vary from person to person. Moreover, if these methods were employed in a test –re- test situation, it is not possible to quantify the reliability correlation coefficient. However, as Li and Wainer (1998) state, it is important to ensure the research method measures in the same way whenever it is used. I am therefore confident that by interviewing I will be measuring the same concept throughout the research. Thus, the measure of homogeneity is not dependent upon psychometric measurements and it may be argued that biographical research can measure the same construct in an internally reliable way (Buse 1996). However, researchers such as Martella et al. (1999) and

Coolican (2009) are of the view that narrative research lacks distinctive quantitative rigor and the same extensive degree of objective analysis.

Osborne (2004) advocates that biographies are unlikely to be objective or detached. This is in my view an accurate assessment of this type of research. However, I see this within biographical work as strength, as the interviewee can draw upon their own life experiences and theorise from them. Erben (1998) argues that interpretation of biographical data involves deductive logical theorisation. This involves postulating and generating inferences upon tentative grounds which are suitably cautious and not making leaps beyond the data. Gilles (2009:115) summarises:

Just as biographers bring different perspectives to the lives they are writing about so the reader's response to different forms of life writing will be coloured by their own experiences and knowledge.

Reliability is a key factor in producing reliable academic research. Bell (2005:117) states: 'Reliability is the extent to which a test or procedure produces similar results under constant conditions on all occasions.' The results would be similar on repeated occasions of re-telling experiences and discussing viewpoints are unlikely to change, as one cannot alter the past. However, what may change is an opinion over time, which is a variable I does not have control over. A potential way around this is to employ ethnographic research, which for the scope of this book would not be applicable.

Cohen et al. (2007) state that story telling within educational research is often a neglected area, which they argue would be employed to a greater extent as it can focus upon exploring the meanings of lives, within their cultural settings and traditions and point to valuable new insights about how people make sense of their educational experiences. Ethington (2004:226) states that: 'storytelling in research can lead to new understandings, insights and revelations...'

Roberts (2002:8) is of the opinion that:

Life stories commonly refer to 'real' events and experiences... Nevertheless, how these events are perceived and selected (even chronologically reordered or changed over time) and placed within understandings of the individual life.

These points are emphasised by Zinn (2004) who has conducted research which highlights how life history such as past experiences affects the story told. In biographical work it is important to exercise reflexivity and not to highlight from an emotional perspective a set of stories which distort the truth about lived experiences. In the light of this I asked all participants to adopt, as far as they were able, a reflexive approach. Gilgun (2010:1) states: 'I believe that all researchers, no matter which methods and perspectives they use, must be reflexive if their research is to be useful.' This involves thinking critically, honesty and openly throughout the research process, which is specifically pertinent in the analysis stage, which I shall now discuss.

3.5   Analysis of interview biographical research data

Bazeley (2009:59) writes: 'Qualitative analysis is about working intensively with rich data.' In so doing I should go through a process of considering different aspects of the biographical account. Erben (1998) argues that four key stages are involved in the analysis of biographical research. The first stage is the specific events relating to a person's actions as well as their thoughts. The second stage is the contextual nature of the data, such as a person's occupation, interests, economic circumstances, educational achievements and so forth. The third stage is societal context – meaning the wider aspects of a person's life. This may as Browne (2009) notes include social, geographical, political and religious aspects of the wider community. Stage four refers to the impact of documentary sources, such as interview transcripts, records and diaries, both of a personal and public nature which can triangulate the data helping to develop a holistic understanding of a person's biographical experiences. Furthermore, within these four stages Erben (ibid) notes that cultural systems impact a life, with reference to the continual changing of values, within the context of the self. Chronology impacts upon a person's experiences, referring to important public and private events occurring within a life time (Baehr 2011). Finally, rehearsals are the refining of the data which has taken place in the four stages (specific events, local context for events, societal context and documentary sources). Erben (ibid) proposes that these various stages of the schema require Is' emphasis in the analysis process.

In terms of the analysis of interviews, it is pertinent to note that as Robson (2002) states the generalisability of biographical qualitative data to the wider audience is a contestable issue. Moreover, Ercikan and Roth (2009) are of the view that a representative sample, encompassing a cross-section of views should be used if the data is generalised beyond the single case study. However, within biographical research this may not always be possible, as a small number of people are interviewed, in depth, rather than a quantitative approach such as a questionnaire or experiment. These may gather more numerical data but forfeit the compendium of the richness of detailed responses, as these are not primarily part of this methodological approach. Moreover, Hesse - Biber and Leavy (2004:49), feminist researchers, argue: 'Quantitative research has provided statistical data clearly revealing oppression not previously recognised.' However, within their research, they suggest that the revelation of oppression becomes more apparent through biographical research. The qualitative approach, through biographical work, offers the opportunity to focus upon the reasons for the occurrence of exclusion, rather than the quantitative statistics of prevalence discussed in the introductory section and Appendix 1.

When analysing participant perspectives of exclusion, I have scrutinised the interview schedule data through implementing a process of coding; sorting the information into themes and theorising what it suggests. Coding is designed to enhance accuracy in analysis and promote accessibility. Denscombe (2006:184) explains: 'Each line in the transcript is given a unique line number, so that parts of the data can be identified and located precisely and accurately.' Efficient and meaningful interpretative coding can be beneficial in the analysis stage (Kitchen and Parker 2011). Bernard and Ryan (2010:275) state: 'As coding categories emerge, the next step is to link them together in theoretical models around a central category that holds everything together.' Grbich (2009) reinforces this point; narrative data can be reduced by grouping and linking ideas into categories. However, I found that not all themes will fall into specific categories (Mishler 2000).

Furthermore, I have primarily implemented the process of multilayered analysis as a way of exploring the variety of meanings that words may carry (Cohen et al. 2007). To take this to a logical conclusion; interpretation and analysis are intertwined, thus multiple levels of analysis can be formulated, affecting the derived meaning (Goodson and Anstead 2012). The interpretation of a theory is a hermeneutical principle which also raises issues such as validity, primarily associated with this type of research. Ricoeur (1978:135) makes a relatable point, '...the two main problems of hermeneutics: that of the status of written texts versus spoken language.' He further assesses the position of explanation and interpretation in text analysis. Moreover, this raises questions over how valid and trustworthy sentiments may be and the premise they are founded upon. In this research I have looked at written sentiments from staff and students relating to the causes of the exclusion and the aftermath of it. I have then compared that to the verbal accounts given by participants, identifying that which occurs in the wake of exclusion. Scott and Usher (1996) identify that internal validity is reflected within a person's sense of truth and reality. Therefore, one interpretation of interview data vary from another, due to the values a person possesses and the worldview they hold to. Altrichter et al. (2008) suggests that within action research, the use of a 'critical friend' can cross-check interpretation. Although the work is biographical by nature, I find Altrichter et al's sentiments a valid way of managing issues surrounding the cogency of the inferred deductions, as deliberations can be made as to how something has been interpreted. Therefore, I used a 'critical' friend, another member of staff, acting as a researcher to help me to complete this stage of analysis.

Yin (2009:70) explains the importance of listening to information as well as correctly interpreting what was said and the way in which it was spoken:

Being a good listener means being able to assimilate large amounts of new information without bias. As an interviewee recounts an incident, a good listener hears the exact words used by the interviewee (sometimes, the terminology reflects an important orientation), captures the mood and affective components, and understands the context from which the interviewee is perceiving the world.

When conducting interviews and subsequently analysing the responses, I need to be aware of the key issues raised by Yin (ibid). Firstly, interviewers should not project biases in their responses or questions. Secondly, interviewers should listen to the precise words the interviewee uses as well as the manner in which they were spoken. The third point is the interpretation should be contextual and take account of the interviewee's paradigm. Arthur et al. (2012:6) describe a paradigm as: '...a particular way of seeing the world...'. Hesse- Biber and Leavy (2004) define a paradigm in terms of a metaphysical set of beliefs for interpreting the world and their situatedness within it. This will be important to recognise, especially when conducting and analysing interview data with both children and adults. Young people may see the world in a different way to an older person, especially if they feel a 'victim' of society or the systems within it. Furthermore, the codes of language they use may vary from adults; a potential divide in the type of language used between the working and middle class may be apparent (Giddens 2009). I was therefore mindful of these matters in the phraseology of questions and in the interpretation of the language used in the responses given. I shall now specifically address the outcomes of this research.

Chapter 4 Research Data and Analysis

4.1 Introduction to the chapter

This chapter is about what has been found out as a result of the biographical research into school exclusion as a means of exploring the impact of professional practice. I shall critically evaluate my enquiry, with specific reflection upon the methods used to investigate exclusion and inform the development and impact of the educational practice in shaping the school exclusion policy.

For the purpose of this study I have used pseudonyms as a way of protecting the identity of the participants. Within the chapter I address the data that has been obtained from interviewing staff and students about their experiences in relation to exclusion. In so doing I seek to give students an opportunity to share their experiences and a platform from which their voice is heard. In addition, I interview some members of staff to seek to understand their perception of school exclusion. This gives staff the opportunity to discuss how they feel about the use of exclusion as a sanction.

4.2 Interviews with staff and students

To foreground this work I shall give a thumbnail sketch of the student. Glen (pseudonym) is a boy who lives with his mother and has infrequent contact with his biological father. He lives in a small house near to the school in an area of high social deprivation.

The National Research Council (1999:48) notes:

Students who live in high- poverty and culturally diverse experience conditions at home, at school, and in the community that correlate with low academic achievement. The conditions endemic in many urban areas- high concentrations of poverty, family instability, crime, unemployment- complicate the process of education enormously.

Glen when interviewed said that he had been temporarily excluded from school due to his continual disruption. This is significant as it may be questioned what is 'disruption'? (O' Regan 2007). This is a subjective term which can be used for a range of behaviours. Rogers (2005) argues that 'disruption' is an umbrella term for inappropriate behaviour. Ruddock and McIntyre (2007) suggest that punishments can be unhelpful as they reduce interactions with students and may affect their self- esteem. As a critique to these remarks, they are generic and no formal experiments are cited to link self –esteem and exclusion. In Glen's case he informed me that during English he got bored, he was in the 'bottom set' and felt like a failure. Alexander- Passe (2010:268) suggests that from research findings those with learning differences can have poor self- esteem and can even suffer with depression: '...depressives feel dyslexia affects their life much more, they feel more helpless, less angry and feel more rejected from their peers than non-depressives.' Alexander- Passe (ibid) cites a number of qualitative and quantitative studies, in which he interviews people with depression and learning difficulties as well as those who have a low self-esteem. As a result, the work indicates a link between low self – esteem and finding school too challenging. However, in the conducting of the psychometric tests, there are no confidence intervals/ bands, which Graf (2005) suggests makes the validity and reliability of a test questionable as ascertaining the 'true' score of a participant is tentative.

During the interview it appeared that some of the work Glen was given was too difficult for him, at one point he said 'what's the point?' This comment referred to him bothering with school. Bennett (2010) argues that students should see the value of work and that it is of most benefit when time is taken to tailor it to their needs. To critique Bennett's (ibid) notion that a curriculum addressing the needs of an individual and by raising the standard of the lesson this will alleviate boredom is refuted by Turner (2011), who suggests that this is simplistic in its reasoning and impractical in its employment; highlights a more specific approach to managing a child's needs is required, such as whole class multisensory teaching, the use of ICT and age appropriate resources. However, Dix (2010) notes that regardless of specific provision there are likely to be children who are challenging in behaviour. Arnot et al. (2007) argue that through consultation with learners, their research reveals that a number of students felt that they had little control over their learning. Mc Namara (2002:114) states: 'The pupils' interest, motivation and rate of learning improved as they were encouraged to create and describe their own methods and solutions to mental maths problems.' As a practice this approach may not suit all types of learner. For example, Muijs (2011) found that some children enjoyed having the teacher set them challenges, rather than generating their own.

The interviews highlighted that Glen appeared to desire help, although he may not admit this, he also seemed to want to take control of his learning and make choices. Galvin (1999:145) states: 'The class should have some part in deciding what needs to be done.' This applied to Glen may allow him to make some decisions, which can be ratified by the teacher. A problem that became apparent was that Glen's perception of the teacher was that they did not care about him and were unwilling to help him access the curriculum as they felt he was a 'nuisance.'

Kinder and Wilkin (1998) suggest that dissatisfaction and disengagement need to be tackled by pupil conferencing, listening to the learner. Glen's self- esteem appeared to be low and he said that he was isolated and felt lonely 'without mates' who would 'hang around with him.' From Glen's home life, he said that most evenings were spent with his mother and when he went out he would end up in trouble. These sentiments infer that Glen was frustrated and when he went out with his friends he 'let off steam' perhaps out of inward tension and did things which were criminal or nuisance type behaviours (Reevy and Frydenberg 2011). Glen shared that he felt unhappy at school and wanted to leave. These sentiments concur with Cooper (2002) who notes that young people who were dissatisfied with school and had been excluded were likely to want to leave school. Thambirajah et al. (2008) argue that students who are unhappy at school over a sustained period of time can become 'school refusers' and feel personally 'attacked' by criticisms of their peers or by their teachers. Mc Sherry (2011:114) on her self-management of behaviour sheet asks: 'can accept discipline without arguing or sulking.' On one occasion Glen was excluded for swearing at his Maths teacher because she was disciplining him and asking him to do something he felt he was unable to do. Glen argued that he felt victimised and 'picked on.' Therefore, he had reacted badly to the teacher's request to comply with instructions and received a three day exclusion. Bruce and Pine (2010) argue that the type of reaction Glen gave needs to be measured against the task. Reflecting upon whether it was too challenging for him and subsequently setting him up for failure. However, Maasz and Schloglmann (2009) notes that Maths can be difficult for some people but is essential for life and therefore work should be challenging. A more balanced argument may be that the teacher needs to consider the task, Glen's capabilities and pre-empt possible behaviour difficulties (Kyriacou 2009, Hart et al. 2011). Chaplain (2003:4) argues the following points for practitioners to consider:

The advantage of using anticipatory strategies (such as seating arrangements, removing temptation, clear rules) as opposed to deflection tactics (such as deliberately ignoring behaviour, praising peers, invading personal space) or reactive strategies (such as warnings, sanctions, exclusion) is the first are far lower profile than the other two and therefore less damaging to the teacher-pupil relationships.

From interviewing the teacher, Mr Smith (pseudonym) explained that Glen's behaviour had deteriorated over the last few months and his attitude towards school was poor. This may be a result of lots of 'reactive strategies' employed in managing Glen's behaviour. Subsequently, Glen had been involved in low level disruption and more recently incidents of higher levels of disruption and acts of defiance. Crone et al. (2010) notes that the categorising of behaviour can be a complex task. However, by doing so it is possible to ascertain whether or not exclusion is necessary. Low level disruption, according to the school, involved deliberately taking long periods of time to complete tasks, talking at inappropriate times, kicking under the table, interrupting the learning and wandering around the room. High level disruption, according to Mr Smith involved vandalism, out right repeated refusal to comply, bullying and severe disruption to lessons (verbally or physically). Mr Smith explained that teaching Glen over the last two weeks had been 'challenging' and he had exhibited continual low- level disruption. Moreover, Mr Smith found Glen disengaged and unmotivated. The example cited above, the swearing incident was a summary of how Glen felt about the work. Mr Smith was of the view that swearing was not to be tolerated and Glen deserved to be excluded. However, this response is subjective and reflects the viewpoint of Mr Smith. Perhaps if another member of staff were interviewed they would argue that exclusion for swearing may not be the most effective solution? Gray (2002) advocates that every day is a new day in terms of a pupil's behaviour and sanctions should not be implemented which effect the child after the period in which they have infringed the rules.

Gray (ibid) further suggests that using foul language is an expression of frustration and emotion. Other theorists, such as Burnham (1993) argue that it may be a sign of gaps within the vocabulary. Hunt and Maloney (2006) take the perspective that swearing is 'joyful.' The division between ideas about swearing make the issue of whether to exclude a child for swearing a controversial one. Munn (2009) reports that the use of exclusion in relation to swearing is a significant cause of suspension. The Deputy Headteacher involved in the exclusion process informed me that Mr Smith had been fully supported in disciplining Glen and exclusion was used for incidents involving foul language being directed at a member of staff.

The research identified from Mr Smith that Glen had been struggling to access the curriculum in class despite having differentiated work. DENI (2006:1) defines differentiation as: 'the process whereby an attempt is made to provide learning experiences which are matched to the needs, capabilities and previous learning of individual pupils'. Moore (2000:144) states:

Differentiation must be embedded in all aspects of teaching and learning. The principle of differentiation is fundamental to the success of mixed ability teaching and work should be carefully matched to the students' attainments and abilities (Glazzard 2016). Practically differentiation for every lesson may be extremely difficult to implement (O'Hanlon 1996).

Pennington et al. (1998) argues that differentiation within the curriculum varies from school to school. If differentiation is implemented efficiently pupils can have greater opportunities to access the curriculum. Simpson and Ure (1994) report that differentiation was not implemented in many primary and secondary schools, which gave sufficient opportunities for those with specific needs to be able to understand the task. However, this report is dated and may not reflect current practice, therefore I shall cite Dunn (2011) who suggests that the mark of an outstanding teacher is one who knows the children within his or her class and differentiates. Turner (2011) found that recent research into differentiation found that a significant number of schools were ineffective in this area. My research suggested that the school was seeking to enhance the provision of differentiation. Mr Smith was of the view that Glen needed booster sessions and 'catch up' groups. However, he felt unwilling to give up his time for Glen who sometimes did not work very hard in lessons. During the exclusion Mr Smith sent home some work for Glen to complete. After the exclusion Glen had only partially completed the tasks Mr Smith had set. This was followed up with Glen's parents. Roffey and O'Reirdan (2003:5) are of the view:

We may not be able to do much about the causes of unwanted behaviour but we can do something about what is happening now. In order to do this, it is essential to formulate some idea of what is maintaining or, indeed, modifying the behaviour. Meeting with families would normally be part of the process gaining additional information which may be useful. As well as finding out about any concerns they may have, parents will be able to give their perspective and also valuable information.

As a result of meeting with Glen's mother and her partner as well as a separate meeting with his father, each person was able to share their concerns about why Glen had been excluded and why work sent home was incomplete. Glen's mother explained that she was unable to 'force' Glen to complete the work and he could be stubborn when he refused to do something. The school suggested the withdrawing of privileges, which as his mother agreed to do. However, Glen appeared disengaged with school and felt that Mr Smith should not have got the senior management team (SMT) involved and felt that the exclusion was unjust and unfair. Parry- Mitchell (2012) argues that school exclusion should be avoided as it creates a sense of injustice and can detrimentally impact upon a student's emotional health, making them angry or upset. To critique these sentiments, Parry- Mitchell (ibid) approaches the subject of exclusion from a standpoint which is to avoid the use of exclusion. In his book he makes the case for anti- exclusion policies, without offering a balanced argument for possible alternatives. Moreover, Parry- Mitchell (ibid) has substantive gaps in his synthesis of literature and fails to critically synthesise a range of viewpoints. Furthermore, his work has been published by perhaps a less highly regarded publishing house among scholars, Lucky Duck and therefore may not have been subject to rigorous analysis.

From analysing the interview Parsons (2011) offers a pertinent point from biographical research with students. He argues that young people can become detached from school, not enjoy it and behave inappropriately if they feel they have been unjustly treated. During the interview Glen explained that another child, Billy (pseudonym) had been pinching and kicking him and Mr Smith only noticed when he swore. Glen felt that the exclusion should also have been directed at Billy as he was specifically involved in this incident resulting in the exclusion. Lawrence (2017) notes that often incidents go unpunished if they are not seen, which in turn can trigger a reaction which is then seen and subsequently punished. Thus, within this case the punishment is implemented upon the reaction rather than the cause of the reaction. This means that sometimes punishments are 'unfairly' given and exclusion can be used inappropriately. Perhaps it may be argued this was the case here, as Glen was not the only child involved in the disruptive behaviour culminating in a more serious incident? Moreover, the triggers of this case could be further investigated.

During the interviews I also spoke to another child, Katie (pseudonym) who had been threatened with permanent exclusion after fighting. Katie is young for the year and has recently lost her grandmother, whom she was close to. Katie has evidently taken this badly as she was emotionally attached to her. Since this event Katie's behaviour has declined and she has been involved in some recent incidents of violence and school refusal. Katie lives with her father and mother, about a ten-minute journey away from the school in a private estate. Katie's parents are going through some marital issues and have been into school recently inferring that they may separate. Katie has refused to speak about how she feels in relation to this matter and the loss of her grandparent. Instead she looks upset and angry and appears to vent this upon other students. As Katie will not cooperate with pastoral support provision, she has recently been informed by the headteacher that she is on her final warning and any further incidents of violence, severe disruption, abuse to staff or students and so forth would result in her expulsion.

When interviewing Katie about her experiences she stated that she was innocent in the event which had occurred resulting in a fight. Katie suggested that she had sought to calm the situation down by going over to Chontelle (pseudonym) and seeking to reason with her. Katie further informed me that Chontelle slapped her and dug her nails into her arm, showing me the scars. During the interview Katie protested her innocence and noted that Chontelle and Alex (pseudonym) were to blame and they had not been excluded but given detention. The seemingly double standards appeared to Katie to be unfair. She felt that she should have not been temporarily excluded and given another warning, as Chontelle and Alex had got a detention instead of an exclusion. This is an example in which exclusion was used for one child and not another. It appears to be unfairly used against Katie and not the others involved in the incident. Arnold et al. (2009) interviewed students and parents about school exclusion. The research includes one student called Letita who felt that the school had let her down and not supported her and was too quick to exclude her. This example cited has a similarity to Katie's story, in which she appears from her reasoning not to have been supported or listened to. Donovan (1998) suggests that sometimes a sense of unfairness can be evident if someone is excluded and someone else involved in the incident is given a lesser punishment. This creates a sense of injustice and the person may become embittered towards the school and headteacher.

When speaking to the Special Educational Needs and Disability Coordinator (SENDCO) she informed me that the headteacher used exclusions sparingly for the most serious breaches of the school rules. Owen (1998) suggests that positive approaches to behaviour management are effective, reducing the need for exclusion. This appears a policy the management were seeking to adopt. However, Katie had infringed the rules on multiple occasions and was well known to Mr Buckle (pseudonym), the deputy headteacher. According to the SENDCO Mr Buckle was monitoring Katie's behaviour, whereas Chontelle and Alex were not currently on report (a system of monitoring behaviour by SMT). Schunk et al. (2010) write that report systems can be used as a way of monitoring behaviour and motivation. However, within this can I would question the effectiveness of this approach, as it appears to have been interpreted in a negative way by Katie. Therefore, in the school's view the use of exclusion in this instance was as a result of Katie's actions, becoming involved in disagreements between two other girls.

The SENDCO explained that part of her role was speaking to students who were on the 'borderline' of exclusion or had been excluded and needed re-integrating. This work included arranging programmes of activities and setting small and manageable targets for these students. The SENDCO was also involved in monitoring report cards for which Katie was on. Edwards (2011) argues that the Special Educational Needs co-ordinator SENCO is a prominent member of staff in helping students with special and behavioural needs. This can act as an important safeguard for managing inappropriate behaviour, ensuring other senior staff are available for other aspects of the day to day running of the school. As a senior member of staff the SENDCO would be directly accountable to the assistant headteachers and would regularly feedback issues and concerns that had been raised. Hallet and Hallet (2010) argue that the description of the SENCO as a member of SMT is a result of flaws within the system. However, it is not my purpose to discuss these perceived flaws, which would deviate from my analysis of the SENDCOs responses to this research project. Ekins (2011:128) notes that the role includes:

> Develop and provide regular information to the headteacher and governing body on the effectiveness of provision for pupils with SEN and / or disabilities to inform decision making and policy review.

Moreover, the SENDCO appears to be a key member of staff in ensuring students are helped to avoid exclusion. The SENDCO highlights issues which have arisen from pupil consultation and helps to form an action plan for dealing with potential problems. In like manner, the special needs area has some isolation desks and members of middle management which are there to help pupils who have been internally excluded or 'removed' from lessons. Cochran-Smith et al. (2008) note that research into student behaviour and resourced provision is an indicator of the school's success in helping students to comply with the rules.

I was fortunate enough to speak with a child, Oliver (pseudonym), who had been sent to this isolation area for infringing the rules. Oliver's background is that he belonged to a family who had moved to the school a year ago, from Lincoln. Both parents worked and had 'highly paid' jobs. Oliver lived in a three-bedroom house close to the school in a more affluent part of the town. As a result of the finances his parents were generating, he had been given many possessions and had access to provisions, such as clubs and sources of entertainment. Giddens (2006:333) argues:

Class continues to exert a great influence on our lives, and class membership is correlated with a variety of inequalities from life expectancy and overall physical health to access to education and well-paid jobs.

Oliver had struggled to settle into the new school. Oliver's response is similar to that recorded by Cooper et al. (2000:1) when interviewing Neil about his move from a Grammar school to a new area: '...Then I had to move... It was getting too much...sometimes I didn't go.' From my interactions with Oliver it appeared that Oliver did not find moving schools easy, similar to the experience of Neil, cited above, he desired to get friends and sought to do this by creating and directing attention towards himself by talking at inappropriate moments. The response of the staff had been to isolate him from the other students. Carlile (2010) notes that exclusion or isolation can be used for 'nuisance' behaviour. It appears that approach was adopted for Oliver. Oliver explained that he had been talking constantly through the input of the lesson. He explained that the lesson was uninteresting and uninspiring.

Further to this he had also incited others to disrupt the lesson and was asked to leave by the teacher. Hansberry (2016) suggest that behaviour such as disruption and encouraging others do break the rules was a reason why some schools had used internal or external exclusion. Oliver had refused to leave the classroom and the SENDCO had been called to ask him to work in the isolation area of the special needs unit. Oliver was very open with me about why he had been sent to the isolation desk but felt that if the lesson was more interesting and the teaching was more stimulating he may not have disrupted the session. Moreover, these sentiments concur with Palaniandy (2009) who suggests that often a well taught lesson with stimulating activities often manages behaviour by 'good' or 'outstanding' teaching. However, Gray (2002) argues that inspiring teaching alone is not always the panacea for promoting good behaviour and avoiding the use of exclusion. Consequently, it is important to remember that Oliver was trying to create attention towards himself, therefore even if the lesson was stimulating he may have disrupted it anyway. However, Oliver appears more engaged in his learning that Glen does. Kantabar and Rae (2010:12) state: 'Another challenge is for those involved in organising the learning process to promote positive engagement before disengagement sets in.' It is important to establish systems which motivate Oliver before he becomes less engaged and pliable to help.

The use of the isolation area appeared to be a prevalent part of school life, as a system of managing or pre-empting poor behaviour initiated by SMT (Davies et al. 2011). Consequently, the unit was also used as a way of preventing the use of external exclusion. This has advantages and disadvantages. First, the advantages are that the students may avoid having an exclusion upon their school record and the school does not need to resort to using a fixed term exclusion (Millimet and Tchernis 2009). Jointly, it provides a structured area for the student to work in, which is monitored by a member of staff (Lall 2004). However, the limitations of this approach are that this may be used instead of an exclusion, when in fact an exclusion should arguably be required, such as incidents of violence or severe disruption (Department for Education 2009). This may put other students and staff at risk of disruption and potential danger from violence or aggression. From my observations the unit appeared to be used effectively, however with one child I saw it could be argued that for this student a fixed term exclusion may have been more appropriate as he continued to behave in an extremely inappropriate way whilst in isolation and disrupt other people in the unit, such as Oliver. Briggs (2011) infers that internal isolation can violate student's rights and may be seen as an 'unofficial exclusion'. On the other hand, Lloyd et al. (2011) explain that measures within the school can contribute to prevent an exclusion occurring. Within this case the isolation of a child, internally prevented them from external exclusion. It could be questioned: which one is more effective? Furthermore, how do staff and students feel about internal exclusion? This is a further line of enquiry which may lead to revisions being made of the exclusion policy and school effectiveness (Yu and Thomas 2008).

I was able to speak to one student about why he felt he had been sent to the unit. Jamie (pseudonym) explained that he was angry with the school as he perceived that they had let him down. King (2011) writing about biographical research into student's experiences of exclusion noted that some of them felt isolated and angry and had a feeling of injustice. Jamie's sentiments support King's research as Jamie suggested that some of his teachers were 'rubbish' and had contributed towards him obtaining poor grades. He was of the opinion that they did not care about how they taught the subject and just gave him lots of questions to complete from the board, textbook or from a worksheet. Dunn (2011) suggests that the outstanding practitioner is a lively and enthusiastic teacher, who carefully plans and implements exciting and varied lessons and demonstrates pastoral care for the students. Perhaps this is not Jamie's perception of his teacher? However, it may be that despite the work of the teacher Jamie is still disengaged? Moreover, he now took pleasure in disrupting the learning as he perceived that the lessons were uninteresting and some of the staff did not care if he did well or not. Browne (2009) from analysing student behaviour noted that some of the most severe forms of disruption were linked to when students did not like the teacher they were taught by. In the remarks Jamie gives it is clear that he has interpreted that the teachers he has dislike him and therefore he chooses to behave inappropriately when taught by them. Jamie stated that during Science lessons he would 'muck around with the equipment' and not do what he was supposed to do. Furthermore, in Maths he said that some of the work was hard and pointless and had no relevance to real life situations. Rogers (2015:114) states the need for teachers to explain the learning objective and subsequent activities in the light of everyday relevance:

One of the most basic aspects of effective (and competent) is that the teacher explains the purpose and relevance of what they are teaching and the particular learning tasks that flow from them.

From these sentiments Jamie appears to be 'switched off' from school and has subsequently adopted learned behaviour patterns of disruption (Steer 2009, Bear 2010). Jamie appeared deeply hurt and felt that he has been badly treated and subsequently has performed poorly in the tests. Black et al. (2009:31) describe some exams as: '...narrow high-stakes summative tests...' These exams, as the 'stakes' are, appear high can be a significant pressure upon an individual, especially if when they receive their results they have not done as well as they hoped or were predicted (Assessment Reform Group 2002). Perhaps school exclusion may not be the answer for Jamie, as this may drive a larger wedge between him and the education system? I would postulate that an intensive support programme, building self- esteem may be more beneficial in this instance and reflecting upon how he may enhance his test scores in future, such as exam technique revision.

It appears that Jamie may also have a low self- esteem in that he manifests little respect for himself and others and finds curriculum access complex (Miller 1994). For the purpose of this work I will adopt Sutton and Stewart's (2011:49) definition: 'Self – esteem refers to the value we attach to ourselves- our personal estimation of our worth as a person.' The use of an educational plan, which incorporates designated time with the pastoral support teaching assistant is being reviewed in terms of its efficiency to promote positive behaviour (Hollis 2005). Kearney (2011) suggests that support structures within school can provide stability and help for a child at risk of expulsion. Within this case these sentiments may be considered pertinent to Jamie's needs. However, some children may not respond, in the sense of improving their behaviour, to support structures (DENI 2006). This experience is similar to the research discourses by Arnold et al. (2009) in which Chip felt that the school had let him down and not supported him and was too quick to exclude before interventions had had time to be effective. Jamie and others like him are currently a concern for the headteacher and the school policy. When dealing with Jamie the school may need to consider how Jamie is feeling as a result of his exclusion (Quibell 2006).

Jamie appeared to be unhappy with the school and was angry at the times in which he had received a fixed term exclusion. Jamie stated:
Schools crap cos they wanted me out... excluded for my behaviour, Mr Winder hates me... What good is it anyway? They just don't like me, its s**t! Didn't even do much.

From these sentiments it is evident that Jamie feels dissatisfied with life at school, assuming that the staff dislike him as a person, rather than some of the behaviours he manifests. It is perhaps needful that Mr Winder (pseudonym) or another member of key staff in dealing with Jamie discuss that they do not feel a grudge towards Jamie rather they dislike the way he behaves at times. Through doing this separation is made between 'you are a very rude and naughty boy' to 'that behaviour was rude and naughty.' Thus, the behaviour is an act which is separated from the person (Grossman 2003). Docking and Mac Grath (2002:7) state:
While some teachers personalise the situation by readily talking of 'problem pupils' or pupils that are 'naughty', 'disruptive', 'disturbed',

'devious', 'troublemakers', 'disaffected' and so on, others prefer to talk in terms of individuals' problem behaviour and its effects.

Palaniandy (2010) argues that understanding student perception is important in developing trust and positive behaviour. Fox (2001:4) argues: 'Every child needs to feel valued. You need to develop positive relationships with those children who find it hard to behave or settle to learning.' In this case if Jamie's misconceptions are challenged then Jamie is more likely to realise why he was excluded and not to take the issue personally. However, I would question the validity of Palaniandy's remarks as although an appreciation of trust is important it will not generate within itself positive behaviour. Sometimes over familiarity in professional relationships can breed contempt (Taylor 2005). Wallace and Gravells (2007) argue in relation to mentoring that a balance between professionalism and allowing your personality to show is an effective way of promoting a positive, working relationship. Newburn et al. (2005:1) summarise:

Mentoring generally involves establishing a relationship between two people with the aim of providing role models who will offer advice and guidance in a way that will empower both parties.

From the interview with Jamie he stated that he felt that this sanction had not helped him to become better behaved or to reform his character. This is a concern as the current exclusion policy is geared towards using exclusion as an ultimate deterrent / sanction, which in Jamie's case has not seemed to have worked. Hyams- Parish (1996) reflecting upon exclusion suggests that if a student does not improve their behaviour as a result of exclusion, this was not a beneficial course of action to take. Jamie expressed disappointment with the school as though they had given up on him. From the interview with Jamie he noted that some of the staff used to shout and sigh when they dealt with him. He also suggested that some teachers appeared to 'hate' him. From analysing these sentiments it is clear that Jamie has a number of substantial issues which require attention and supportive intervention work may be required. This interview has been significant in developing professional practice as I now have a greater understanding of Jamie's needs and can suggest the implementation of changes through consultation with Jamie and other disaffected students. This adopts a similar approach to Kay Kinder's work (1998) in which she looks at pupil dissatisfaction and seeks to address their issues through narrative research (Kinder 1998). Thus, she discovered students who were unhappy with the education system and sought to make recommendations for improving professional practice through her research. These ideas have helped me to bring various considerations to the headteacher, for example, what are the steps before exclusion? Is there a system or process which can be used to engage those who are not currently engaged in school life? Perhaps policies need to be re-thought to integrate personalised learning opportunities, which stimulate students? (Hopkins 2008). To summarise Mac Grath (2000:4) makes the emotive cause for learning and satisfaction at school. The argument is based upon two perceptions of progress and happiness and therefore has flaws. However, the point raised is pertinent to studying the students I have interviewed, particularly in relation to dissatisfaction and the learning experience and the subsequent progress they may make:

> ...unless pupils are comfortable in the classroom, unless they have friends and are happy enough with the relationships in the class and unless they feel sufficiently at ease in the school they will not learn. In other words, unless their emotional well-being is considered progress will be severely hampered: children's feelings count.

Finally, I interviewed the headteacher of the school. This interview was specifically important as he is authorised to issue school exclusions. Correspondingly, he has a considerable say in the formation of policies to which the staff and students are expected to comply with. Mr Barrington (pseudonym) stated during the interview that the use of exclusion was a 'last resort' after many other attempts have been used to curb a student's behaviour. However, sometimes, as money was tight, teaching assistant posts made redundant, the availability of help was decreased. Thus, sometimes exclusions could be used more than in previous years (such as 2015, before the funding crisis in UK schools). Cooper (2002) suggests that many headteacher's do not use exclusion in the way Mr Barrington states, as an 'ultimate sanction'. Which as Cooper (ibid) argues can lead to confusion and tension. Mr Barrington argued that exclusion was sometimes used as a severe sanction such as in cases of violence or extreme disruption. This implementation is in line with government guidance (Great Britain Department for Education 2009). It may be asked what is meant by the 'ultimate sanction'? Frederickson and Cline (2009) are of the view that other 'ultimate sanctions' are more appropriate. By contrast, Bracher (2003) argues that schools should be permitted to have and use exclusion if they wish to as the 'ultimate sanction.' Mr Barrington made an insightful comment noting that exclusion was not used in his school often and he preferred to use pastoral support plans and the unit as ways of managing challenging behaviour. Furthermore, the plans helped those with learning difficulties who may exhibit inappropriate behaviour as a result of their condition (Turner 2011). Individual Education Plans (IEPs) defined by Blamires et al. (1999:3) 'the IEP communicates targets to be met and anticipated learning outcomes to all involved in its delivery.' The Education Health Care Plan (EHCP) replaces many IEPs and refines targets across a range of needs. Nettleton (2015) in the context of the EHCP, suggests that students with special needs may find curriculum access problematic as well as finding behaving within the parameters of school rules problematic and therefore are at greater risk of exclusion. Mr Barrington echoed these sentiments by explaining that children with SEN are more likely, when looking at National Trends, likely to be excluded. This concurs with literature that suggests those with special needs are eight times more likely to be excluded than those without specific needs (Asthana 2010). However, he stated that the school tried to implement support for children at risk of exclusion.

The headteacher argued for some children this is an effective sanction, which 'shocks' them back and reforms them. However, he argued that for others exclusion is less effective in terms of being an effective sanction. Mr Barrington stated:

> Let's be clear from the beginning exclusion is a response to the 'end of the line' being reached. I would only use it after all other avenues have been explored and that without success. However, I won't tolerate disruption and those that do this see me or my Deputy. Our pastoral support plans and specific provision have been set up as ways of helping those with learning difficulties and as a way of managing those who are at risk of exclusion. ...For some children an exclusion works and it is right but for others it pushes them further away from a system they are already fighting... But as you know the whole school policy is subject to significant revision shortly...

Mr Barrington explained that exclusion could be controversial and some headteacher's were 'anti exclusion' whereas others actively supported it and would implement this. Searle (2001) suggests that there is a compelling argument that the education system has been established upon exclusion. Additionally, Kantabar and Rae (2010) note that support for disaffected students should be more prevalent in the education system rather than exclusion. They highlight that support which focuses upon the triggers of disengagement whilst taking into account the situatedness of the person within a culture and context. However, additional support costs money, time, resources and potentially the training of specialist staff, which as Nind et al. (2003) state are in short supply in schools. Wright et al. (2000:6) comment: '...reduced resources in schools for the support of children with behavioural difficulties...' As a result of this, Osler (2003) argues that some schools seek to permanently exclude a child. However, as Osler (ibid) notes, this does not solve the problem or detract the responsibility for educating these children, it just moves the 'problem' somewhere else. Rowley (2009) also argues that schools should avoid moving children to other schools by the use of exclusion. However, this argument appears to be based upon unsubstantiated foundations and does not consider the impact of exclusion. Perhaps a more significant point is made by Smith (1998) when he identifies that exclusion can cause detriment to children's emotional health. However, this still does not take into account the impact of the child being at school and disrupting the education of others and the emotional labour this creates for the staff (Skiba 2001). Dunham (1992:3) state: '...stress is concerned with both pressures and reactions and also with coping resources...' Travers and Cooper (2006:18) state: 'sources of teacher stress, e.g. disruptive pupils.' Lazarus and Folkman (1984) highlight the stress disruptive behaviour can cause to teaching staff and note that stress can cause teachers health problems. By contrast to Rae (ibid) McNamera and Moreton (2001) suggest that exclusion used proportionately and fairly is appropriate regardless of other circumstances. To synthesise these notions; what is meant by fairly or proportionately? One headteacher's idea of fair may be different to another (Carlile 2010).

Exclusion, in Mr Barrington's view, can also cause problems at home such as supervision issues of minors, which may inconvenience parents / primary care givers. These remarks are echoed by Cooper (2002) who suggests that exclusion can have a detrimental impact upon domestic life. Cooper (ibid) uses interviews which suggest the strain that has been placed upon families that have had to look after their children during an exclusion. As Hallam and Rogers (2008) suggest, this can put potential barriers up between the school and home and cause difficulties in effective liaison. However, Knowles (2011) asks the perennial question: should exclusion be debated as a result of this? One child Mr Barrington told me a similar account to my own experiences, about was where he excluded a child for a week, for fighting and disruption. However, the single mother claimed she had no means of looking after her son. Therefore, she brought him back into school and went off to work. This evidently caused problems as the child was in school and the school had no way of contacting the parent. Mr Barrington explained in these situations exclusion needs to be considered carefully, reflecting upon the potential good it may do and weighing it up against the potential problems.

In like manner, Mr Barrington highlighted that exclusion was effective if parents supported the exclusion. If they did not, this could lead to the child being allowed to play at home instead of work. These sentiments concur with Clemson and Clemson (1990) who argue that exclusion is most effective when parents are supportive in their involvement of the process. Mr Barrington was of the opinion that in these cases exclusion was assessed and sometimes internal isolation could be more effective than one off site. Martin et al. (1999) suggests that if a student is excluded they may begin a downward spiral, which results in the individual getting into further trouble. By way of critique Martin et al. (ibid) make general remarks and do not suggest empirical evidence to ratify their emotive claims, their sentiments may be judged within the light of this. A further critique of my own objection may be to say as Thomas and Pring (2004:203) say: 'A lot depends on how one interprets the word 'evidence.'' The research indicated that Mr Barrington was of the view that sometimes students who are excluded either on a fixed term basis or permanently are more likely to become disengaged and be 'failed by the system.' Thus, exclusion in Mr Barrington's view has both potential pitfalls as well as positive aspects which need to be carefully synthesised before implementing.

A final point Mr Barrington made, which appears pertinent in the use of exclusion was that a decision taken to exclude temporarily (over five days) or permanently can be challenged by parents and the governors meet to discuss this (see Appendix 5).

Mr Barrington noted that the Pupil Disciplinary Committee, made up of three to five governors would meet and discuss with the parents and child the reasons for the exclusion and would either uphold them or re-instate them. If the parents disagreed with the decision they could ask for an independent appeal hearing. Kearney (2011) argues that this process allows for greater transparency and towards a system promoting inclusive education. This, however, raises questions about what is meant by inclusion, should all children be educated, regardless of need or behaviour in one place? (Warnock 2005). Moreover, Wearmouth et al. (2005: 3) state: 'Inclusion is a term which lacks adequate theorising or consensus about what it means in practice.' The Learning Trust (2004:6) offers these remarks:

> Sometimes "inclusion" is seen as something that works against, rather than with, the promotion of a positive learning environment. In other words, the inclusion of pupils in the mainstream who have challenging behaviour undermines the learning opportunities of others.

Therefore, does the appeals process actually promote inclusion or 'drag out' the inevitable?

Mr Barrington further explained that an appeals hearing was a 'long winded process' and if successful the student would be allowed back to school. This, he argued could be difficult and needed to be sensitively managed. He noted that after an exclusion the child may not be able to settle back into the school and moving on and making a fresh start may be more beneficial to the student. However, Mr Barrington said that sometimes re-integration can work. Wright et al. (2005:15) notes from their research that: 'Many interviewees explained that they were ostracised when they attempted to reintegrate in schools.' This included being branded as a trouble maker, being ignored by some staff and students and given further punishments. Mr Barrington concluded by explaining that permanent exclusion was a carefully considered option that the school did not take lightly. From these sentiments exclusion appears to be a controversial area and requires sensitivity and informed decisions to be made. I would conclude by questioning the appeals procedure, whether this disempowers Mr Barrington or whether this is an essential human right and a promoter of inclusion? Mansell (2010) reports that Lewis Hamilton was wrongly accused of assault by mistaken identity and subsequently excluded from school. The appeals panel heard and overruled on a case of injustice. If this appeals panel was not in place Hamilton may have been wrongly excluded. Mansell (ibid) suggests that his human rights may have been infringed if this complaints procedure was not in place. However, on the other hand, does the panel have the right to overrule the head of the school? Dyke (2011:4) writes that the government plans to abolish independent complaints panels in an attempt to 'give the power back to the headteacher' and create a greater sense of justice. These are open ended matters which are not easily resolved.

4.3 Conclusion to the chapter

In summary, I have found out through exploring and investigating educational practice that some students find school exclusion a difficult experience and have reacted in a number of ways, including feeling angry and upset as well as having a sense of injustice at the exclusion. It has been of importance to remember these sentiments when adjusting the exclusion policy. Some of the interviewees gave examples of why they were excluded. These included continual and / or severe acts of disruption, violent conduct or abusive language. From the interviews a key emerging theme was that some students were disengaged with school and others found the lessons 'boring' and subsequently lost interest and resorted to being disruptive. As a result of this the headteacher has commissioned senior staff to inspect lessons and use lead learners and visiting leading teachers to improve the quality of lessons, ensuring teaching is at least 'good' in all classes. This has further led to departmental changes and has helped to redefine class rules, the behaviour policy and has meant less exclusions being given. The rationale was working from the 'grass roots' upwards. If teaching was enhanced, boundaries understood, the behaviour code of conduct revised then learning would be much more meaningful and the use of exclusion reduced. Verhoeven (2012) suggests that the reasons for doing research are to benefit practice, which has been a significant part of this work. Moreover, this work has enabled me to critically evaluate the system of school exclusion, which has informed and developed practice.

A further point I noted was that the unit and special needs centre is used to support students with specific learning difficulties as well as provide a place of support for those who are on report or close to exclusion. This unit is monitored by senior staff and students who are significantly at risk of expulsion. Wilson (2005) writing about the use of a unit and solution – focused therapy for those at risk of exclusion explains that this process aims to support and help individuals work through problems by seeking to address their needs. It may be argued that the unit seeks to do this. From my research I found that many members of staff were willing to adopt a similar approach to that of Wilson's findings, based upon resolving matters. This is now something which is to be written in the school policy, the use of solution-based practice, whereby individuals who are at risk of exclusion are helped to 'overcome' their difficulties.

I have adopted a critical understanding of the enquiry through using biographical research methods and have found out about school exclusion from the perspective of some staff and students. The information gathered is insightful, sophisticated, informing practical situations, which is both original and unique and contributes towards the body of knowledge in relation to what is currently known and understood about school exclusion. Arguably, this data has helped to understand the nature of exclusion, give an idea of emotional responses to it as well as to give an overview of one school's use of exclusion. Moreover, the features and characteristics of exclusion have been clearly manifest as responses have outlined a number of potential concerns with the use of exclusions and the use of internal isolation (the unit). The sentiments of the headteacher have shed light upon the potential dilemmas associated with exclusion, such as considering how beneficial exclusion is to managing inappropriate behaviour. This in the context of this project has enabled amendments to be made to the possible reasons for exclusion section within the school policy, which are to be further discussed within the staff training days, planned as a result of this research project.

Chapter 5   Conclusion

5.1   Introduction to the chapter

This chapter concludes what has been learnt from this investigative enquiry. It appraises the research methods used and summarises what has been found out and evaluates what has been done as a result of the project. Thus, it discusses the implications of what this book has had upon the school exclusion policy. Finally, the chapter critiques the work and suggests the limitations of the study and offers further lines of enquiry, whilst noting the original contribution this project has made to enhance the knowledge of exclusion.

5.2   Appraisal of the research methods

Harper (2004) notes that data from school based research can substantially help to develop a school policy. These sentiments could be applied to the outcome of this work. There have been significant implications of using interviews to conduct the research, as they have been useful in providing a tool to hear the voice of staff and students in relation to school exclusion. The specific benefits of using interviews relate to the rich and substantive data that have been obtained from such an approach (Creswell, 2013) As part of this research, ethical issues played an important part; these included gaining informed consent, acting with integrity to ensure participants are protected from harm. Consequently, confidentiality and the safeguarding of data were important considerations to ensure participants were protected and detrimental reprisals did not occur. Additionally, the interpretation of data was conducted in an ethical way to ensure accurate renditions of what has been said. This is important as the policy, which is being reviewed is using data obtained from this book to address issues relating to if and when to use exclusion.

This book has explained that biographical work can research the experiences of both pupils and staff within the exclusion process. Biographical inquiry has offered specific doors of opportunity to give a voice to the voiceless, highlighting pupil and teacher experience, inequalities, flaws in the system and so forth. Biographical research has provided a platform for voices from the margins to be heard. It allowed individuals to share experiences of how school exclusion has affected them.

I have used a process of analysis which has sought to consider the story told in an holistic way, with reference to a person's situatedness and contextual position. This has helped when analysing the responses given by students like Glen, Katie, Oliver and Jamie. It is pertinent to remember that the school is situated within an area of social deprivation and both students have specific difficulties with school life. Therefore, their sentiments need to be considered within the light of this; the staff responses are positioned within their belief system about school exclusion and relate to the school they are currently working in as well as the paradigm they adopt.

5.3 Summary of the work and an evaluation of the implications of this research in informing and developing educational practice

This work has analysed the implications of biographical research within the context of school exclusion. It has explored and researched exclusion within a school context as a means of investigating and developing professional practice. This book has contributed to the proposed changes that the school believe are necessary within the exclusion policy. Moreover, through implementing this research project I have gained data which has led to a whole school review about the nature, feature and characteristics of school exclusion. These amendments will reflect upon how staff and students feel about exclusion. For example, questions have been raised about the suitability of an exclusion as a sanction. In addition, students' feelings have been considered throughout this book, thus the policy will now embed the research data and reflect upon these matters before an exclusion is given. The policy is now to contain specific instances in which exclusion may be considered viable as well as alternatives which may be employed prior to an exclusion being issued. Thus, this has positively addressed the previous shortcomings of the old policy and sought to be specific and objective in when exclusion may be seen as appropriate. Subsequently, clear guidelines are given for when a student may be internally isolated. This avoids ambiguity and excessive use of the unit. It also empowers staff, who have not used it before, to do so, in avoiding disruption to their class and promotes, as Rogers (2015) argues, for greater colleague support.

From using the data collection and analysis methods I employed to conduct the research I have found out that some students are disengaged with school and find learning uninspiring. This may be due to having specific learning difficulties, finding accessing the curriculum difficult or to having a low self-esteem. Some of the respondents felt that their exclusion was unjust and unfair. It is clear that the research has highlighted inconsistencies in the use of exclusion. For example, staff previously did not have a policy for specific instances whereby exclusion is required and therefore any decisions are made subjectively. Therefore, this work has enabled a list of possible incidents to be devised and staff are now to refer to it before calling a member of senior staff. In turn the SMT are to use it to judge whether an exclusion is necessary.

I have also critically interpreted the descriptions of why exclusions were applied; mainly for violent behaviour and disruption. Moreover, the interviews suggested that students were excluded for physical or verbal abuse. Equally, I have identified that head teachers are at liberty to judge a situation such as serious inappropriate behaviour upon its merits and exclude as they determine the need to. However, it has been argued that this can cause problems because prior to this research there was no specific uniform policy which identifies when exclusion should be used and when alternatives would be more appropriate. This may lead to varied interpretations of events, depending upon a variety of factors such as the paradigm and the policy that the head teacher adopts. This was a pertinent area which the interviews highlighted.

The exclusion policy will now reflect staff viewpoints as well and the policy is due to be re- evaluated with further staff input in an in-service training day within the next month. A summary of this research will be presented by myself. Within this presentation, time will be set aside for staff to be asked about their opinion of a whole school amendment to school exclusion. Some of the themes raised in this work indicated that exclusion was necessary for acts of defiance or severe disruption or fighting. The headteacher noted that pastoral support plans and the use of the inclusion centre / unit are resources which can be made use of to prevent having to externally exclude. Davies (1999:27) reporting about exclusion within schools in Liverpool writes: 'All teachers in these schools seem to attempt to take on a pastoral responsibility for disaffected pupils.' In the light of my own research the school policy has now been re- written to contain support interventions prior to or after an exclusion is given. This is now seen as an integral feature of good practice as is as a direct result of speaking to the staff and students and reviewing the literature.

The special needs area and attached unit are regularly used by middle and senior management overseen by the SENDCO. This unit provides a tool to seek to prevent exclusions occurring, as it can internally isolate students who have been asked to leave their lessons. The SENDCO is directly accountable to the SMT and oversees the day to day running of the unit as a provisional resource. She is also used to setting targets for those who are at risk of exclusion. Perhaps the suggestion in the next meeting will be to capitalise upon this resource or consider more carefully the way in which is it used? At the moment it appears to be a 'sin bin' rather than a specific resource which the school could use more effectively, to help students like Glen or Katie.

Mr Barrington mentioned appeals panels, which are employed to offer second, more impartial decisions to be made, based upon objective criteria. Conversely, this could lead to disempowerment of the head teacher in the case of a decision being overturned. Alternatively, it could be said that the system offers a structure of democracy. Biographical research can provide openings for individuals to express their views upon key note points, such as the impact an exclusion has had upon them, how they feel about the provision they are being offered as well as their opinions about the appeals process. On a personal note, I hold the view that the head teacher should be empowered to make ultimate decisions, in the case of severe disruption to their school. However, at present I feel the system of school exclusion locally and nationally, needs revision, as the criteria of an exclusion can be made subjectively; causing confusion and problems for the students, parents and professionals. Narrative research has the potential to reveal how others feel about the current system of school exclusion. Within this book feelings of resentment, frustration and anger have been examples of how some students feel when excluded. This has been carefully considered in the section of the school policy in which examples of when exclusion are to be given is mentioned.

An underlying element of this book is the discussion of the implications of biographical work and exclusion within the 21st century, asking the question: does the system need to change or the people within the system? Therefore, I postulate that there have been great benefits of biographical methods for generating qualitative data relating to the nature, characteristics and features of exclusion, through listening to the varied experiences and perspectives of both staff and students alike. Biography and life narrative has helped to shed light upon an exclusion to provide a more profound and rich picture of this problematic area in education so that better and more well -informed decisions are made about whether to exclude or not.

5.4   Limitations of the research and possible further lines of enquiry

This work has made a significant impact in shaping the policy for the school I work in, especially in relation to the exclusion policy. The gap between research and the classroom can sometimes be made. However, as Hendrick and Macpherson (2017) argue, that all research should ask in the title of their book: 'what does this look like in the classroom?' Moreover, embedding the findings into practice and re-forming the policies is a key way of answering this question, which is already starting to occur. This book encourages you to take the sentiments of those interviewed and ask similar questions to elicit feelings about how practice may be enhanced in your educational institution.

However, a caution of this work is that one has to interpret the statistical data of the aetiology of exclusions and the patterns thereby in the light of Weale's report, that the figures for exclusions may not be indicative of the national picture. Moreover, Weale (2016) argues that statistics are likely to be more than five times higher than qualitative datasets report. However, I have made original, insightful and sustained cogent arguments, offering a critical and sophisticated analysis of research within this field. I have drawn directly from the data and presented my findings to senior staff and then later to all the teaching staff. However, as with any research project there are limitations and areas which could be developed further. For example, this project could be further extended or developed as a comparison between two schools. This would offer a perspective of exclusion from different schools and even catchments, providing opportunities for comparisons in how the exclusion policy is managed. A potential further line of enquiry would be to develop biographical research into school exclusion with a larger sample size. This may allow for an ever -greater depth of study, providing more participants perhaps offering disparate data. However, despite these limitations and potential projects, this book offers a powerful insight into school exclusion and has impacted upon my educational practice. It has demonstrated a critical understanding of the research methods pertinent to this enquiry. Moreover, the book has identified the methodological decisions underpinning the selection of these data collection and analysis tools, as well as noting the ethical considerations which exist. I have designed and critically applied data collection and analysis to a key area of educational enquiry, which is current and of substantial impact upon informing and developing new, original insights into practical situations. I find a resonance in the following sentiments and conclude by noting Ruddock and McIntyre (2007:154): 'The experiences of the pupils, teachers and the schools with which we worked suggested that consultation can have a 'transformative potential.'' This is particularly important as there are a limited supply of books and other literature which are not at least a decade old, and to some extent do not reflect some of the current issues facing schools. This book aims to highlight a range of issues against the backdrop of the new government guidance for exclusions (in draft format- Summer 2017) and the present school funding crisis of 2016 onwards. What occurs in the wake of these matters, is yet to be seen but could lead to schools increasing the number of exclusions due to the lack of finance, experienced staff and resources they have to deal with challenging students.

Appendices

Appendix 1. Biographical research into the prevalence of exclusion

The prevalence of school exclusion has opportunities for quantitative and qualitative research. Through interpreting numerical data a researcher can form a judgement based upon the cases and the pervasiveness of exclusion. However, as an Appendix to this book I suggest that although exclusion can be viewed statistically, by implementing biographical research a clearer understanding of the individuals involved and the specifics of each case could be achieved.   In so doing this may help to develop a more sensitive approach to exclusion and subsequent policy/ strategies.

In terms of quantitative data Gordon (2001) suggests that sharp increases in school exclusions occurred in the 1990s. He notes that the prevalence is most significant in English and Welsh schools and most apparent in Secondary schools. A further point that he adds is that black children are most frequently excluded. Despite Gordon's claims, he does not quote any statistics, or reference his sentiments, leaving the reader to draw their own conclusions.

Figure 1.1   The number of permanent exclusions between 1989 and 1998 (Parsons 1999:39).

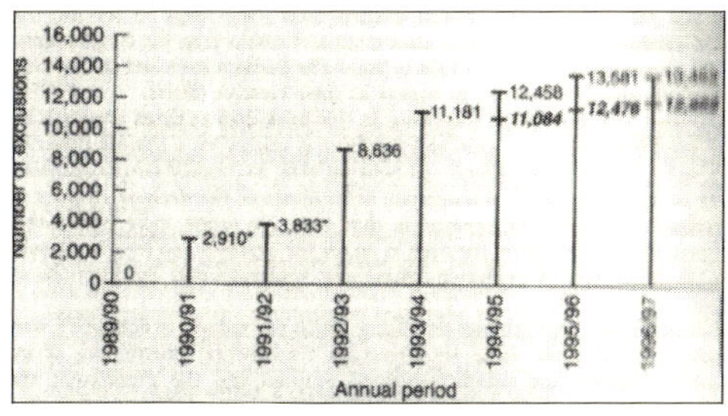

It is evident that between this period, 1989 and 1998, the number of exclusions increased significantly, peaking around 1995 and 1996 to approximately 13 000 permanent exclusions from England's schools.

Data from the former DFES (Department for Education and Skills, 2005) suggests that in the years 2002 and 2003, there were 9880 permanent exclusions in all types of schools, representing a 0.13 percent of all pupils in schools. This, they underline, is an increase of 6 percent on the year 2001, but a decrease of 20 percent since 1997 and 1998. Thus, more contemporary prevalence figures indicate a decline in exclusion rates. Data in 2009 from the Department for Children Schools and Families (DCSF 2009:1) noted:

In 2007/08 there were 324,180 fixed period exclusions from state funded secondary schools compared with 363,270 in the previous year. This represents a decrease of 10.8 per cent. There were 43,290 fixed period exclusions from primary schools, a decrease of 5.3 per cent, and 16,350 fixed period exclusions from special schools, a decrease of 1.5 per cent. Across all school types, the number of fixed period exclusions decreased by 9.8 percent.

Eastman et al. (2011:11) summarise the statistics of school exclusion in 2009 to 2010:

> Latest figures from 2009/2010 show there was an estimated 5,740 permanent exclusions, and 331,380 fixed-term exclusions, amongst a pupil population of approximately eight million.

Contemporary analysis suggests: 'The overall rate of permanent exclusions has increased from 0.07 per cent of pupil enrolments in 2014/15 to 0.08 per cent in 2015/16.' (National Statistics, Gov.uk, 2017).

Even more recent figures indicate a spike in school exclusions. Bloom (2017) postulates that initial permanent exclusion rates have 'rocketed' around 300% since 2015 (Bloom 2017).

There are a number of factors which may impact upon the prevalence of exclusions (Parsons 1999:25). These include poverty, health, race, criminal activity, deviance, home circumstances and whether the role model in the home is it predominantly male or female. Becker (1963) in his work entitled 'Outsiders' looking at social deviance made the point that boys from predominantly middle-class families became less involved in the criminal justice system than those from 'slum areas' (p.12). For the purpose of this books Appendix, I will mention that this is an avenue of potential research. However, its scope is beyond the limitations of this Appendix.

Appendix 2. Some reasons for pupil exclusions

Table 2.1 Summary of reasons for exclusions within the Secondary sector for 1997, percentage equating to the number exclusions per annum in inner and outer London: (SEU1998:10).

Reason	Percent
Bullying, fighting, assaults on peers	30.1
Disruption, misconduct	17.0
Verbal abuse to peers	14.9
Verbal abuse to staff	12.0
Miscellaneous	8.1
Theft	5.5
Defiance	5.0
Drugs, smoking	4.0
Vandalism	2.4
Physical abuse/assault upon staff	1.2

The categories in the above table are broad; however, despite this a general pattern can be seen, giving some insight into the reasoning behind the head teacher's decision to exclude. The SEU (ibid) data suggests a large proportion of exclusions occurred as a result of violence. However, it is uncertain as to the specific nature of the offences, without qualitative sentiments supporting the statistics. The miscellaneous section is ambiguous in identifying the nature of the infringement. Research (through biographical means) into the lives of those who have been excluded may reveal motives for the occurrence of the exclusion and could help to understand how they felt about the exclusion and the aftermath thereof. Exclusion is often dealt with by government documentation as a statistic and that by employing biographical research a better understanding of the individuals involved and the specifics of each case could be achieved (Cooper 2002).

Appendix 3. Biographical research into the exclusion of pupils with SEN

This Appendix explores the relationship between special needs and exclusion within biographical research, this is pertinent as it will be established, that those with SEN are more likely to be excluded than those who do not have specific needs (educational, emotional or behavioural needs). I have chosen to focus upon SEN as some quantitative data, explained in this Appendix, suggests those with SEN are more likely than those without special needs, to be excluded, thus, it is worthy of exploration. This includes a discussion of the reasons for and against exclusion of those with complex needs as well as seeking to clarify what may be meant by this term. Moreover, it highlights the opportunities that exist within biographical research to elicit how students with SEN feel if they have been excluded. Narrative enquiry gives opportunities to understand how parents of children with SEN feel if their child has been excluded. It also allows staff to give their point of view on this matter, such as why they choose to make the exclusion.

Firstly, those diagnosed with SEN have risen significantly within the last ten years (Palmer 2006). This may be partially due to increased awareness of SEN. Palmer (2006:3) states that 'There are a number of learning difficulties which didn't even enter the public consciousness until the late twentieth century.' Other reasons include genetic influences as well as environmental factors (Beckett 2007). The nature - nurture perennial issue is however beyond the scope of this book. The question posed is: should a school exclude children with specific needs, such as emotional and behavioural problems? Exclusions within the primary sector saw a rise of 18 per cent between 1995 and 1996 and in the secondary schools, 80 per cent of those excluded were between the ages of 12 and 15 (Rendall 2001). These exclusionary rates varied from school to school but were highest in London and outer London areas, and peaked in places of social deprivation or amongst those with special needs. Roth et al. (2010) argues those with Autism Spectrum Disorders (ASDs) and SEN are likely to have behavioural needs, which are unlikely to be accommodated for in the many mainstream schools. Subsequently, these children are more likely to face permanent exclusion than their peers. Biographical work into the experiences of those excluded with SEN could prove enlightening and such sentiments may concur with Rendal (ibid) and Roth et al. (ibid) relating to the significant proportion of those with SEN who are excluded. Issues such as equality of opportunities may emerge as well as sentiments which reflect upon the current provision for those with specific needs.

In the summary of the Social Exclusion Unit's report (SEU 1998:12, 13) the pupils, who were highlighted as the most likely to be excluded, were white teenagers with special needs, Afro – Caribbean pupils and looked after children, in care. The report indicated that, 'Children with special needs are six times more likely than others to be excluded.' These sentiments are strengthened by Vasager (2009), who states that those with SEN are 8 times more likely to be excluded than those without specific needs. Thus, since the SEU report (ibid) there have been an increase in exclusion rates for those with SEN, according to Vasager (ibid). Biographical research into head teachers' reasons for the exclusion of those with SEN could help to clarify why a disproportionate number of pupils with SEN are excluded. Head teachers may address in an interview issues such as exclusion being a reaction to severe behaviour being manifest, which the school could not tolerate. Further to this they may highlight matters such as access to funding and specific provision and the limitations of the school budget.

An alternative perspective is that schools should be able to exclude those with SEN without feeling a sense of disservice to them. This may allow them to have an education which meets their needs and help them to access the curriculum. Lovey et al. (1993:17) explains that those who are disaffected should have their needs met by 'education otherwise,' for example in referral units or specialist schools, where resources and arrangements are in place for such children. Eastman et al. (2011:127) are of the view:

We argue in this report that children and young people should be supported as far as possible to stay within the mainstream education system. We recognise, however, that the needs of a minority are likely to be so severe and complex that they would be better met in an alternative educational setting.

Conversely, why should schools have to permanently exclude children in order to obtain appropriate provision for those with specific learning difficulties? Biographical work may allow those with specific needs the opportunity to be heard (Arnold et al. 2009). Alternatively, their parents or carers could offer their opinions upon the exclusion process (Armstrong 2006).

The government has recently proposed an Education Bill which will make it more difficult to exclude pupils in which the school would be responsible organising and funding alternative education (Paton 2011). Biographical work may offer the opportunities to discuss the impact of how staff feel about such proposed legislation (Fangen et al. 2010). Research can also delve into a person's experience, listening to the decision- making processes they have undergone in determining the most effective provision for those with SEN (Mc Kenney and Reeves 2012; Graves and Duncton, 2017). For example, by listening to a child's perception of their learning differences, the way they perceive education and their plans for the future, a researcher could inform the decision maker of how they understand what the most effective course of action may be (Laar 1996). This may also offer the opportunity to discuss learning styles and the impact of them upon their work (Reid 2005). Biographical research can use such data to understand the specific needs of an individual as well as inform successive lessons, seeking to potentially increase inclusion and decrease the need for an exclusion to be made (Skidmore 2004, Sayed 2007).

Appendix 4.   Towards a definition of inclusion

The terms 'inclusion' and 'exclusion' are broad and most clearly understood when both are defined. The expression 'inclusion' is often used but how much is actually understood by this? Grondin (1994), with reference to syllogism and hermeneutical principles explains that interpretation and inclusiveness vary from one person to another. When inclusion is considered, some argue it is a desired state with implications that are impractical in the light of the many pressures upon the practitioner (Croll and Moses 2000). Mah (2009:1) states: 'The inclusive classroom is a wonderful concept, but also a complex day- to – day challenge for teachers.' On the other hand, it may seem to be that inclusion entails so called exclusion as part of its process, either actively or as a by- product of promoting positive learning environments without disruption (Alur and Timmons 2009). I find a resonance in Reid's sentiments, Reid (2006) argues that inclusion does not just happen and there are a number of unanswered issues related to inclusive education. From the outset I note that by definition and practice these matters are divisive, therefore biographical studies by its nature and reason of the selected area of writing offers the opportunity to make personal accounts known.

The terms 'inclusion' and 'Special Educational Needs' (SEN) are often used interchangeably (Frederickson and Cline 2009). Slee (2011) makes the point that inclusion is based upon the perception of SEN; and subsequently challenges practitioners to be reflexive in their approach to their practice. To reflect upon the past perceptions of SEN, The Warnock Report (1978) emphasised the continuum of needs, not specifying between the severity of needs and explaining that these may change over time (Lunt and Norwich 2002). Dash (2010) advocates that those with SEN will inevitably be more likely to be successful, if assessed, with a view to arranging appropriate provision to support their needs. This may as Puri and Abraham (2004) note, lead to enhanced understanding of behavioural, emotional or physical needs, which without such intervention may be a contributory factor in causing an exclusion to be made. Knowles (2011:114) suggests: 'School leaders establish the ethos that either welcomes or sidelines disabled children and children with SEN.' Inclusion therefore, takes into account the varied needs of all children and seeks to meet them (Mitchell 2004). School leaders should evaluate the benefits and limitations of exclusion upon the promotion of inclusion (Artiles et al. 2011, Ryan 2006).

Appendix 5. Protocol in School Exclusion

This Appendix explains one school policy in managing an exclusion from school. Kelly (2011:1,2) writes in the school policy:

The Head Teacher must inform the Governing Body if a pupil is being excluded for more than 15 days in any one term. Pupils can be excluded for one or more fixed periods, which when aggregated, do not exceed 45 school days in any one school year. All parents/carers have the right to make representations to the Governors' Discipline Committee about their child's exclusion. The Committee does not have to meet by law to review the exclusion unless the pupil has accumulated at least 16 days exclusion in any one term unless the parent wishes to make representations about an exclusion of fewer days. The Governors do not have the powers to direct reinstatement for exclusions under 6 days but they should still consider the views of parents, if that is their wish. Parents will be invited to attend the meeting, along with the child if this is appropriate, so that Governors can take account of parents' views, alongside those of the Head Teacher, when considering the exclusion. Governors must have regard to current Department for Education guidance on exclusion and have the power to uphold or reduce the length of the exclusion but they cannot recommend that it be extended. There are no rights of appeal for fixed period exclusions. From the 6th consecutive day of the exclusion the school is compelled to provide provisions for fulltime education.

References.

1998. Social Exclusion Unit consultation on school exclusions, Great Britain, Learning and Skills Development Agency.

2005. Statistics of education: permanent exclusions from maintained schools in England, Norwich, The Stationery Office.

N. R. C. 1996. Improving Student Learning Washing DC: National Academy Press.

Alexander-Passe, N. 2010. Dyslexia and depression: the hidden sorrow: an investigation of cause and effect, Hauppauge, N.Y., Nova Science.

Altrichter, H., Posch, P. & Somekh, B. 2009. Teachers investigate their work: an introduction to the methods of action research, London, Routledge.

Alur, M. & Timmons, V. 2009. Inclusive education across cultures: crossing boundaries, sharing ideas, Los Angeles, Sage.

Anderson, G. L., Herr, K. & Nihlen, A. S. 2007. Studying your own school: an educator's guide to practitioner action research. London, Sage.

Armstrong, S. 2006. Perspectives on punishment: the contours of control, Oxford, Oxford University Press.

Arnold, C., Yeomans, J. & Reeves, S. S. 2009. Excluded from school: complex discourses and psychological perspectives, Stoke-on-Trent, Trentham.

Arnot, M., McIntyre, D., Peddler, D. & Reay, D. 2007. Consultation in the classroom: developing dialogue about teaching and learning, Cambridge, Pearson Pub.

Arthur, J., Waring, M., Coe, R. & Hedges, L. (eds.) 2012. Research Methods and Methodologies in Education, London, Sage.

Artiles, A. J., Kozleski, E. B. & Waitoller, F. R. 2011. Inclusive education: examining equity on five continents, Cambridge, Education Press.

Author. 2010. Special needs pupils account for seven in 10 permanent exclusions from schoolchildren with special educational needs just short of statement level most likely to face exclusion. The Observer, 19th December 2010, p.23.

Atkinson, D. 1997. An auto/biographical approach to learning disability research, Aldershot, Ashgate.

Atkinson, R. 1998. The life story interview, London, Sage.

Baehr, J. S. 2011. The inquiring mind: on intellectual virtues and virtue epistemology, Oxford, Oxford University Press.

Basit, T. N. 2010. Conducting research in educational contexts, London, Continuum.

Bathmaker, A. & Harnett, P. (eds.) 2010. Exploring Learning, Identity and Power through Life History and Narrative Research, London, Sage.

Bazeley, P. 2009. Qualitative data analysis with NVivo. London, Sage.

Bear, G. G. 2010. School discipline and self-discipline: a practical guide to promoting prosocial student behaviour, London, Guilford.

Becker, H. 1967. Whose side are we on? Social Problems 14, 239-247.

Becker, H. S. 1963. Outsiders. Studies in the sociology of deviance, pp. x. 179. Free Press of Glencoe: New York; Collier-Macmillan

Beckett, C. 2007. Human growth and development, London, Sage.

Bell, J. 2005. Doing your research project: a guide for first-time researchers in education, health and social science, Maidenhead, Open University Press.

Benjamin, S. 2002. The micropolitics of inclusive education: an ethnography, Buckingham, Open University Press.

Bennathan, M. & Boxall, M. 2008. Effective intervention in primary schools: nurture groups, London, David Fulton.

Bennett, T. 2010. The behaviour guru: behaviour management solutions for teachers, London, Continuum.

Berridge, D., Brodie, I., Pitts, J., Porteous, D. & Tarling, R. 2001. The independent effects of permanent exclusion from school on the offending careers of young people. Research, Development and Statistics Directorate. London: Home Office. RDS Government Statistical Service (GSS).

Black, P. J., Harrison, C., Lee, C., Marshall, B. & Wiliam, D. 2009. Assessment for learning: putting it into practice, Maidenhead, Open University Press.

Blair, M. 2001. Why pick on me? School exclusion and black youth, Stoke-on-Trent, Trentham.

Blake, N. 2003. The Blackwell guide to the philosophy of education, Oxford, Blackwell.

Bloom, A. 2017. Exclusive: Permanent exclusions 'skyrocket' by as much as 300% in a year. Accessed; https://www.tes.com/news/school-news/breaking-news/exclusive-permanent-exclusions-skyrocket-much-300-a-year

Blyth, E. E. & Milner, J. E. 1996. Exclusion from school: inter-professional issues for policy and practice, London, Routledge.

Bornat, J. & Tetley, J. 2010. Oral history and ageing, London, Centre for Policy on Ageing.

Bracher, D. 2003. Pupil exclusion from school: an organisational perspective Bristol: University of Bristol.

Brassey, A. 2010. The management of behaviour disorder in English secondary schools. London: University of London.

Breen, J. 2009. Life histories and biographical research methods. Dublin: School of Social Work and Social Policy, Trinity College.

Briefings, D. R. 2006. Approaches to Differentiation in Primary Schools. Bangor, Co Down: Department of Education Northern Ireland.

Briggs, D. (ed.) 2011. Out of School, Out of Sight: Unofficial school exclusion in the UK London: Lambert Academic Publishing

Brinberg, D. & Kidder, L. H. 1982. Forms of validity in research, San Francisco, Jossey-Bass.

Brodie, I. 2001. Children's homes and school exclusion: redefining the problem, Philadelphia, PA, Jessica Kingsley Publishers.

Browne, J. W. 2009. An educational psychologist's perspective on pupils' learning and behaviour in two secondary schools for emotional and behavioural difficulties. Bristol: University of Bristol.

Bruce, S. M. & Pine, G. J. 2010. Action research in special education: an inquiry approach for effective teaching and learning, New York, Teachers College.

Bryman, A. 2008, 2015. Social research methods, Oxford, Oxford University Press.

Bulmer, M., De Vaus, D. & Fielding, N. 2004. Questionnaires, London, Sage Publications.

Burnham, J. C. 1993. Bad habits: drinking, smoking, taking drugs, gambling, sexual misbehaviour, and swearing in American history, New York; New York University Press.

Buse, A. 1996. Testing homogeneity in the linearised almost ideal demand system, Edmonton, Alta., Department of Economics, University of Alberta.

Cameron, C., Mooney, A. & Owen, C. 2001. Childcare students and nursery workers : follow up surveys and in-depth interviews, Great Britain, Department for Education and Skills.

Campbell, A. & Groundwater-Smith, S. 2007. An ethical approach to practitioner research : dealing with issues and dilemmas in action research, London, Routledge.

Carlile, A. 2010. The causes and effects of permanent exclusion from school [electronic resource] : Policy and practice in an urban children's services department [Online]. London: Goldsmiths. Available: http://eprints.gold.ac.uk/3426/

Carver, C. S. & Scheier, M. 2008. Perspectives on personality, London, Allyn and Bacon.

Chaplain, R. 2003. Teaching without disruption in the primary school : a model for managing pupil behaviour, London, Routledge Falmer.

Charlton, T. & David, K. 1989. Managing misbehaviour : strategies for effective management of behaviour in schools, Basingstoke, Macmillan Education.

Clandinin, D. J. & Connelly, F. M. 2000. Narrative inquiry : experience and story in qualitative research, San Francisco, Calif., Jossey-Bass.

Clemson, W. & Clemson, D. 1990. School Exclusion, Cheltenham, Stanley Thornes.

Clemson, W., Clemson, R. & Clemson, D. 2002. Exclusion - the cost, Cheltenham, Stanley Thornes.

Clough, P. & Barton, L. 1998. Articulating with difficulty: research voices in inclusive education, London, Paul Chapman.

Cochran-Smith, M., Feiman-Nemser, S. & McIntyre, D. J. 2008. Handbook of research on teacher education: enduring questions in changing contexts, London, Routledge.

Cohen, L., Manion, L. & Morrison, K. 2007. Research methods in education, London, Routledge.

Cohen, L., Manion, L. & Morrison, K. 2011, 2017. Research methods in education, London, Routledge.

Cohen, R., Hughes, M. A. & Ashworth, L. 1994. School's out: the family perspective on school exclusion, Family Service Units.

Coolican, H. 2009. Research methods and statistics in psychology, London, Hodder Education.

Cooper, B. 2012. Challenging the qualitative-quantitative divide: explorations in case-focused causal analysis, New York, Continuum.

Cooper, C. 2002. Understanding school exclusion: challenging processes of docility, Nottingham, Education Now.

Cooper, P., Drummond, M., Hart, S., Lovey, J. & McLaughlin, C. 2000. Positive alternatives to exclusion, London, Routledge.

Copeland, I. C. 1999. The making of the backward pupil in education in England, 1870-1914, London, Woburn Press.

Corbin, J. M. & Strauss, A. L. 2008. Basics of qualitative research: techniques and procedures for developing grounded theory, Thousand Oaks, California, Sage Publications, Inc.

Council, B, School Exclusions [Online]. Hove: City House.

Council, D. C. 2012. Exclusion of Pupils from School. Topsham, Exeter DCC.

Council, L. C. 2011. Appealing against an exclusion from school information. Newland, Lincoln: LCC.

Council, N. Y. C. 2012. School - exclusion of pupils [Online]. North Hallerton: NYCC.

Cowley, S. 2003. Sue Cowley's teaching clinic, London, Continuum.

Creswell, J. 2013. Educational Research: Pearson New International Edition: Planning, Conducting, and Evaluating Quantitative and Qualitative Research. London, Pearson.

Croll, P. & Moses, D. 2000. Ideologies and utopias: education professionals' views of inclusion. European Journal of Special Needs Education 15, 1-12.

Crone, D. A., Hawken, L. S. & Horner, R. H. 2010. Responding to problem behaviour in schools: the behaviour education program, London, Guilford Press.

Cullingford, C. 1999. The causes of exclusion: home, school and the development of young criminals, London, Kogan Page.

Dash, L. N. 2010. Education and inclusive development in India, New Delhi, Regal Publications.

Davies, B. 2008. Doing collective biography, Maidenhead, Open University Press.

Davies, D. 1999. Child development: a practitioner's guide, London, Guilford Press.

Davies, L. 1999. School councils and pupil exclusions: research project report, School Councils UK.

Davies, P. M., Popescu, A.-C. & Gunter, H. M. 2011. Critical approaches to education policy and leadership, British Educational Leadership Management & Administration Society.

Dawson, C. 2009. Practical research methods: a user-friendly guide to mastering research techniques and projects, Oxford, How To Books.

Denscombe, M. 2006. The good research guide for small-scale social research projects, Maidenhead, Open University Press.

Denzin, N. K. 1989. Interpretive biography, California, Sage.

Denzin, N. K. 2001. Interpretive interactionism, California, Sage.

Department of Health, E., and Welfare. 1974. The Belmont Report. An ethical framework for protecting research subjects. Crown Copyright, London.

Department of Health, Education., and Welfare. 2011. School exclusion statistics for 2009/10 [Online]. London: Crown Publishing.

Derlega, V. J., Winstead, B. A. & Jones, W. H. 2005. Personality: contemporary theory and research, Wadsworth; London, Thomson Learning.

Dhunpath, R. & Samuel, M. (eds.) 2009. Life History Research. Epistemology, Methodology and Representation Rotterdam, Netherlands: Sense Publishers.

Dix, P. 2010. The essential guide to taking care of behaviour, Harlow, Longman.

Docking, J. W. & MacGrath, M. 2002. Managing behaviour in the primary school, London, David Fulton in association with the University of Surrey, Roehampton.

Donovan, N. E. 1998. Second chances: exclusion from school and equality of opportunity, London, New Policy Institute.

Drever, E. 2006. Using semi-structured interviews in small-scale research: a teacher's guide, Glasgow, Scottish Council for Research in Education.

Dunham, J. 1992. Stress in teaching, London, Croom Helm.

Dunn, D. (ed.) 2011. How to be an outstanding Primary School Teacher, London: Continuum.

Author. 2011. Exclusions: a school's right to decide. Stripping independent appeal panels of their power to order that pupils be reinstated could result in more litigation, not less. The Guardian 21.3.11, p.4.

Eastman, A., Smellie, D., Clark, J., McGrath, G., Collins, J., D'Abbro, J. & Smith, W. 2011. No excuses. A review of educational exclusion. In: POOLE, G. (ed.) A policy report by the Centre for Social Justice.

Education, (The Department for) 2011. Exclusion guidance [Online]. London: Crown Publishing.

Edwards, S. 2011. The SENCO survival guide: the nuts and bolts of everything you need to know, London, Routledge.

Ekins, A. 2012. The changing face of special educational needs: impact and implications for SENCOS and their schools, London, Routledge.

Elton-Chalcraft, S., Hansen, A. & Twiselton, S. 2008. Doing classroom research: a step-by-step guide for student teachers, Maidenhead, Open University Press.

Equality, G. B. 1997. Exclusion from school and racial equality: a good practice guide, Great Britain, Commission for Racial Equality.

Erben, M. 1998. Biography and education: a reader, London, Falmer press.

Erben, M. 2000. Ethics, Education, Narrative Communication and Biography Educational Studies, 26, 379-390.

Ercikan, K. & Roth, W.-M. 2009. Generalizing from educational research: beyond qualitative and quantitative polarization, London, Routledge.

Ethington, K. (ed.) 2004. Becoming a Reflexive Researcher. Using ourselves in research, London, Jessica Kingsley Publishing.

Evans, J. 2010. Not present and not correct: Understanding and preventing school exclusions. London: Barnado's.

Fangen, K., Fossan, K. & Mohn, F. A. 2010. Inclusion and exclusion of young adult migrants in Europe : barriers and bridges, Farnham, Ashgate.

Flick, U., Von Kardoff, E. & Steinke, I. (eds.) 2008. A companion to qualitative research, London: Sage.

Flutter, J. & Rudduck, J. 2004. Consulting pupils: what's in it for schools? London, RoutledgeFalmer.

Foddy, W. 1993. Constructing questions for interviews and questionnaires: theory and practice in social research, Cambridge University Press.

Forde, C., McMahnon, M., MCPhee, A. & Patrick, F. 2006. Professional development, reflection, and enquiry, London, Paul Chapman.

Fox, G. 2001. Supporting children with behaviour difficulties: a guide for assistants in schools, London, David Fulton.

Fraenkel, J. R. & Wallen, N. E. 2008. How to design and evaluate research in education, London, McGraw-Hill Higher Education.

Frederickson, N. & Cline, T. 2009. Special educational needs, inclusion and diversity, Maidenhead, McGraw Hill/Open University Press.

Galvin, P. 1999. Behaviour and discipline in schools, London, David Fulton.

Author. 2009. Teenagers could appeal against school exclusions. The Independent p.32-33.

Geddes, B. 1990. How the Cases You Choose Affect the Answers You Get: Selection Bias in Comparative Politics. Political Analysis, 2, 131-150.

Gedo, J. E. & Gedo, M. M. 1992. Perspectives on creativity: the biographical method, Norwood, NJ, Ablex.

Gerver, R. 2010. Creating tomorrow's schools today: education - our children - their futures, London, Continuum.

Gibbs, G. 2009. Qualitative data analysis: explorations with NVivo, Buckingham, Open University Press.

Giddens, A. 2006. Essentials of sociology, New York, Norton & Company.

Giddens, A. 2009. Sociology, Cambridge, Polity.

Gilgun, J. 2010. The power of the case. Current Issues in Qualitative Research, 1, 3-17.

Gillies, M. (ed.) 2009. Writing Lives: Literary Biography Cambridge, Cambridge University Press.

Girard, P. P., Roy, O. & Marion, M. 2011. Dynamic formal epistemology, Dordrecht, Springer.

Glazzard, J. 2016. Learning to be a Primary Teacher. Northwich, Critical publishing.

Glover, J. 2009. Bouncing back: how can resilience be promoted in vulnerable children and young people? Ilford, Essex: Barnado's.

Goodley, D. 2011. Self-advocacy in the lives of people with learning difficulties: the politics of resilience, Buckingham, Open University.

Goodson, I. 1992. Studying teachers' lives, London, Routledge.

Goodson, I. & Anstead, C. J. 2012. The life of a school+: a research guide, New York, Peter Lang.

Gordon, I. R. 2001. Does spatial concentration of disadvantage contribute to social exclusion? Economic and Social Research Council. Author. 2007. Exclusion in schools. The Daily Telegraph.

Graf, E. A. 2005. Psychometric and cognitive analysis as a basis for the design and revision of quantitative item models, [Princeton, N.J.], ETS.

Graves, S. & Duncton, T. 2017. Behaviour Matters: Monkey Needs to Listen - A book about paying attention. Kindle edition.

Gray, P. 2002. Working with emotions: responding to the challenge of difficult pupil behaviour in schools, London, Routledge/Falmer.

Grbich, C. 2009. Qualitative data analysis: an introduction, London, Sage.

Great Britain Department for Education. 2009. Exclusions from school, London, The Stationery Office.

Great Britain. Department for, Education & Employment 2000. Statistics of education: permanent exclusions from maintained schools in England, London, The Stationery Office.

Great Britain Department for Education and Science 1978. Warnock Report - Special Educational Needs - Command Book 7212 - May 1978, [S.l.], HMSO.

Great Britain. Office for Standards in, E. 1996. Exclusions from secondary schools 1995/96, Great Britain, Office for Standards in Education.

Greene, S. & Hogan, D. 2009. Researching children's experiences: methods and approaches, London, Sage.

Gregory, I. (ed.) 2003. Ethics in Research, London New York: Continuum.

Grondin, J. 1994. Introduction to philosophical hermeneutics, New Haven; London, Yale University Press.

Grossman, H. 2003. Classroom behaviour management for diverse and inclusive schools, Oxford, Rowman & Littlefield Publishers.

Group, A. R. 2002. Testing, Motivation and Learning. Cambridge: Cambridge University Faculty of Education.

Hallam, S. & Castle, F. 2001. Exclusion from school: what can help prevent it? Educational Review, 53, 169-179.

Hallett, F. & Hallett, G. 2010. Transforming the role of the SENCO: achieving the National Award for SEN Coordination, Maidenhead, Open University Press.

Hansberry, B. 2016. A practical introduction to restorative justice in schools. London, Jessica Kingsley.

Hardwick, L. & Worsley, A. 2011. Doing social work research, London, Sage.

Harper, H. 2004. The role of research in policy development [electronic resource]: school sex education policy in Scotland since devolution. University of Glasgow. Available: http://theses.gla.ac.uk/2198/

Harris, D. & Passmore, S. 2009. A common thread: addressing local and government initiatives through high quality pupil and student consultation, Birmingham, Birmingham Health Education Service.

Harris, N. S. & Eden, K. 2000. Challenges to school exclusion: exclusion, appeals, and the law, London, Routledge/Falmer.

Hart, L. C., Alston, A. S. & Murata, A. 2011. Lesson study research and practice in mathematics education: learning together, Dordrecht, Springer.

Hayden, C. & Martin, D. (eds.) 2011. Crime, Anti-Social Behaviour and Schools, Chippenham Eastbourne: Palgrave.

Hendrick, C. & Macpherson, R. 2017. What Does This Look Like In The Classroom: Bridging The Gap Between Research And Practice. Woodbridge, John Catt.

Herr, K. & Anderson, G. L. 2005. The action research book: a guide for students and faculty, London, Sage.

Hesse-Biber, S. N. & Leavy, P. 2004. The practice of qualitative research, London, Sage.

Hobbs, C. 2005. Professional consultation with pupils through teaching about learning: educational psychologists working with pupils to explore their understanding of themselves as learners as they move from primary to secondary school [Online]. Newcastle upon Tyne: University of Newcastle upon Tyne.

Hollis, I. R. 2005. Predicting and preventing behaviour difficulties at Key Stage 3: a study of a mainstream secondary school and three primary schools. Bristol, University of Bristol.

Holmes, R. M. 1998. Fieldwork with children, London, Sage.

Hopkins, D. 2008. Every school a great school realizing the potential of system leadership, Maidenhead, McGraw-Hill/Open University Press.

Hopkins, D. 2008. A teacher's guide to classroom research, Maidenhead, Open University Press.

Author. 2010. South East shows pupils the door. Fixed - period exclusions: percentage of total number of pupils. The TES, p.16, April 2010.

Hunt, C. 2000. Therapeutic dimensions of autobiography in creative writing, Philadelphia, PA, Jessica Kingsley Publishers.

Hunt, M. & Maloney, A. 2006. The joy of swearing, London, Michael O'Mara Books.

Hyams-Parish, A. 1996. Banished to the exclusion zone : school exclusions and the law from the viewpoint of the child, London, Children's Legal Centre.

IPSEA 2001. Responses to the DfES consultation on exclusion appeals panels London: ebusiness.

Johns, C. 2009. Becoming a reflective practitioner, Chichester, Wiley-Blackwell.

Kampwirth, T. J. & Powers, K. M. 2012. Collaborative consultation in the schools : effective practices for students with learning and behaviour problems, Upper Saddle River, N.J., Pearson.

Kane, J. 2011. Social class, gender and exclusion from school, London, Routledge.

Kantabar, P. & Rae, T. (eds.) 2010. Tackling Exclusions: Supporting Disaffected Students, Poole, Dorset: CMP.

Kay, D. & Hinds, R. 2007. A practical guide to mentoring: how to help others achieve their goals, Oxford, How To Books.

Kearney, A. (ed.) 2011. Exclusion from and Within School: Issues and Solutions, Rotterdam, Netherlands: Sense Publishing.

Kelly, S. D. 2011. Exclusion Policy Pamber end, Tadley: The Priory School.

Kember, D. & Ginns, P. 2012. Evaluating teaching and learning a practical handbook for colleges, universities and the scholarship of teaching, London, Routledge.

Kinder, K. & Wilkin, A. 1998. With all respect reviewing disaffection strategies, Slough, National Foundation for Educational Research.

King, H. 2011. Young people's experiences of school exclusion and support from the voluntary sector in England and Wales. York: University of York.

Kirk, J. & Miller, M. L. 1986. Reliability and validity in qualitative research, Beverly Hills, Sage Publications.

Kitchen, J. & Parker, D. 2011. Narrative inquiries into curriculum making in teacher education, Bingley, Emerald.

Kitching, R. C. 2001. Violence, truancy and school exclusion in France and Britain: report of a seminar, Franco British Council, British Section.

Knowles, G. (ed.) 2011. Supporting Inclusive Practice London, Routledge

Kvale, S. 2009. Interviews: an introduction to qualitative research interviewing, London, Sage.

Laar, B. 1996. Effective teaching, Oxford, National Primary Centre.

Lall, M. C. 2004. Exclusion from school: addressing the hidden problem of teenage pregnancy, Sheffield, Sheffield Hallam University, Centre for Regional Economic and Social Research.

Lamb, T. E. 2005. Listening to our learners' voices: pupils' constructions of language learning in an urban school. Nottingham, University of Nottingham.

Lawrence, T. 2017 Practical behaviour management. London, Bloomsbury.

Lazarus, R. S. & Folkman, S. 1984. Stress, appraisal, and coping, New York, Springer.

Letherby, G. 2005. Auto/biographical reflections or 'how who we are affects what we know', York, York St. John College of the University of Leeds.

Li, H. & Wainer, H. 1998. Toward a coherent view of reliability in test theory, Princeton, N.J., Educational Testing Service.

Lim, L. H. 2005. Leadership mentoring in education : the Singapore practice, Singapore, Marshall Cavendish Academic [Lancaster : Gazelle Drake Academic, distributor].

Lincoln, Y. S. & Guba, E. G. 1985. Naturalistic inquiry, London, Sage.

Author. 2008. Tories scrap independent school exclusions appeals The Guardian, September 8th 2008.

Lloyd, G., Stead, J. & Kendrick, A. 2001. Hanging on in there: a study of inter-agency work to prevent school exclusion in three local authorities, London, National Children's Bureau.

Lo, Y. Y. 2010. What happens to classroom interaction patterns and teachers' code-switching behaviour when the medium of instruction changes? [electronic resource] : an exploratory study in Hong Kong secondary schools [Online]. Oxford University.

Lovey, J., Docking, J. W. & Evans, R. 1993. Exclusion from school : provision for disaffection in key stage 4, London, David Fulton in association with the Roehampton Institute.

Lunt, I. & Norwich, B. 1999. Can effective schools be inclusive schools? London, Institute of Education.

Maasz, J. r. & Schloglmann, W. 2009. Beliefs and attitudes in mathematics education - new research results, Rotterdam, Sense Publishing.

MacBeath, J. & Myers, K. 1999. Effective school leaders: how to evaluate and improve your leadership potential, London, Financial Times/Prentice Hall.

MacGilchrist, B. & Savage, J. 1994. The impact of school development planning in primary schools: early findings, London, University of London, International School Effectiveness & Improvement Centre.

MacGrath, M. 2000. The art of peaceful teaching in the primary school: improving behaviour and preserving motivation, London, David Fulton.

Macrae, S. & c, M. J. 2003. Starting young - challenging exclusion in the primary school, Swindon, Economic and Social Research Council.

Author. 2009. Children with special needs are eight times more likely to face expulsion. Times Educational Supplement p.13, July 2009.

Mah, R. 2009. Getting beyond bullying and exclusion: PreK-5 : empowering children in inclusive classrooms. London: Sage.

Author. 2010. Threat hangs over appeals panels for excluded children Tories are keen to get rid of appeals panels, but they are a fundamental right for children who may have been unjustly excluded from school. The Guardian 26.6.10.

Martella, R. C., Nelson, J. R. & Marchand-Martella, N. E. 1999. Research methods: learning to become a critical research consumer, Boston, Allyn & Bacon.

Martin, T., Hayden, C. & Turner, D. 1999. Out of school and into trouble? exclusion from school and persistent young offenders, London, Social Services Research and Information Unit.

Massey, A. & Groves, J. 2011. Best behaviour: school discipline, intervention and exclusion, London, Policy Exchange.

May, T. & Perry, B. 2011. Social research & reflexivity: content, consequences and context, London, Sage.

Mc Namera, O. (ed.) 2002. Becoming an evidence based practitioner, Gateshead, Ashgate.

Mc Sherry, J. (ed.) 2011. Challenging Behaviour in Mainstream Schools: Practical Strategies for Effective Intervention and Reintegration, London, David Fulton.

McAra, L. 2004. Truancy, school exclusion and substance misuse, Edinburgh, University of Edinburgh, Centre for Law and Society.

McKenney, S. E. & Reeves, T. C. 2012. Conducting educational design research, London, Routledge.

McLeod, J. 2008. Learning from the margins: young women, social exclusion and education, London, Routledge.

McNamara, S. & Moreton, G. 2001. Changing behaviour: teaching children with emotional and behavioural difficulties in primary and secondary classrooms, London, David Fulton.

McNiff, J. & Whitehead, J. 2006. All you need to know about action research, London, Sage.

Merrill, B. & West, L. 2009. Using biographical methods in social research, London, Sage.

Mertens, D. M. 2005. Research and evaluation in education and psychology: integrating diversity with quantitative, qualitative, and mixed methods, London, Sage.

Mertens, D. M. & McLaughlin, J. A. 1995. Research methods in special education, London, Sage.

Miller, A. 1994. Successful interventions with difficult pupil behaviour in primary schools: a critique of consultative practice between educational psychologists and teachers from the perspective of applied behavioural analysis, organisational dynamics and attribution. Sheffield, Sheffield University of Sheffield.

Millimet, D. & Tchernis, R. 2009. Estimation of treatment effects without an exclusion restriction: with an application to the analysis of the School Breakfast Program, Cambridge, National Bureau of Economic Research.

Mishler, E. G. 2000. Research interviewing: context and narrative, Cambridge, Harvard University Press.

Mitchell, D. R. 2004. Special educational needs and inclusive education: major themes in education, London, Routledge.

Moon, J. A. 2004. A handbook of reflective and experiential learning: theory and practice, London, RoutledgeFalmer.

Moore, A. 2000. Teaching and learning: pedagogy, curriculum, and culture, London, RoutledgeFalmer.

Mortimore, P. & Sammons, P. 1988. Forging links: effective schools and effective departments, London, Paul Chapman.

Muijs, D. 2011. Doing quantitative research in education with SPSS, Thousand Oaks, California, Sage.

Munn, P. 2009. Behaviour in Scottish schools 2009, Edinburgh, Social Research.

Munn, P., Lloyd, G. & Cullen, M. A. 2000. Alternatives to exclusion from school, London, Paul Chapman.

Nathan, H. 1986. Critical choices in interviews: conduct, use, and research role, Berkeley, Institute of Governmental Studies, University of California.

Nettelton, M. 2015. Special Needs and Legal Entitlement, London, Jessica Kingsley.

Newburn, T., Shiner, M. & Young, T. 2005. Dealing with disaffection: young people, mentoring, and social inclusion, Cullompton, Willan Publishers.

Nind, M., Sheehy, K. & Simmons, K. 2003. Inclusive education: learners and learning contexts, London, David Fulton.

Noffke, S. E. & Somekh, B. 2009. The SAGE handbook of educational action research, London, Sage.

Norbert-Obonyo, K., Ovon-Atia, R. & Apoko-Olara, F. 2001. A review of school exclusion and black children in Bromley and neighbouring areas for Crystal Vision Trust, African Refugee Community Health & Research Organisation.

Author. 2012. Boy in limbo after illegal exclusion. The Guardian, 22nd March, p.7.

Ofsted 2009. The exclusion from school of children aged four to seven London Crown Copyright.

O'Hanlon, C. 1996. Professional development through action research in educational settings, London, Falmer Press.

Oppenheim, A. N. 1992. Questionnaire Design, Interviewing and Attitude Measurement, London, Pinter Publishers.

O'Regan, F. J. 2007. Can't learn, won't learn, don't care: troubleshooting challenging behaviour, London, Continuum.

Osborne, B. D. 2004. Writing biography and autobiography, London, A. & C. Black.

Osler, A. & Vincent, K. 2003. Girls and exclusion: rethinking the agenda, London, RoutledgeFalmer.

Osler, A., Watling, R. & Busher, H. 2000. Reasons for exclusion from school, Great Britain, Department for Education and Employment.

Owen, P. 1998. Turning it around: a practical guide to positive behaviour management in primary schools, Cardiff, Relay Publications.

Palaniandy, S. 2009. A study of student perceptions of teacher characteristics and its influence upon the management of student behaviour in four Malaysian secondary schools [electronic resource] [Online]. Leicester: University of Leicester. Available: http://hdl.handle.net/2381/7854

Palmer, S. 2006. Toxic childhood: how the modern world is damaging our children and what we can do about it, London, Orion.

Parke, C. N. 2002. Biography: writing lives, London, Routledge.

Parkes, B. 2012. Exclusion of Pupils from School in the UK. The Equal Rights Review, 8, 1-17.

Parry-Mitchell, C. (ed.) 2012. The Behaviour Management Toolkit: Avoiding Exclusion at School Bristol, Lucky Duck.

Parsons, C. 1999. Education, exclusion and citizenship, London, Routledge.

Parsons, C. 2011. Strategic alternatives to exclusion from school, Stoke-on-Trent, Trentham.

Author. 2011. Rules change 'will stop schools from expelling the worst pupils.' The Daily Telegraph 3rd January 2011, p.1.

Author. 2012. Children consigned to scrapheap in education 'holding pens'. Schools set up to teach badly behaved pupils are often little more than "holding pens" where children spend time playing pool and searching Face book, a Government advisor has warned. The Telegraph, April 2012, p.12.

Peddler, D. & McIntyre, D. 2007. Improving learning through consulting pupils, London, Routledge.

Pennington, P., Taylor, M. & Lewis, G. 1998. Learning from differentiation : a review of practice in primary and secondary schools, National Foundation for Educational Research in England and Wales.

Piper, H. & Stronach, I. 2004. Educational research: difference and diversity, Aldershot, Hants, England; Burlington, VT, Ashgate.

Popper, K. R. 1992. Unended quest: an intellectual autobiography, London, Routledge.

Popper, K. R. & Eccles, J. C. 1977. The self and its brain, London, Springer International.

Porter, L. 2006. Behaviour in schools: theory and practice for teachers, Buckingham, Open University Press.

Pritchard, A. 2009. Ways of learning: learning theories and learning styles in the classroom, London, David Fulton.

Pryce- Jones, J. & Lutterbie, S. 2010. Why leveraging the science of happiness at work: The happy productive employe. Assessment & Development Matters, 2, 6-9.

Punch, K. 2009. Introduction to research methods in education, London, Sage.

Puri, M. & Abraham, G. 2004. Handbook of inclusive education for educators, administrators, and planners: within walls, without boundaries, New Delhi, Sage Publications.

Radnor, H. A. 2001. Researching your professional practice: doing interpretive research, Buckingham, Open University Press.

Ramalho Fernandes Salgueiro, M. 2002. Distributions of test statistics for edge exclusion for graphical models Southampton: University of Southampton.

Reevy, G. 2011. Personality, stress, and coping: implications for education, Charlotte, N.C., Information Age Pub.

Reid, K. 2006. Truancy and schools, London, Routledge.

Rendall, S. E. 2001. Factors relating to exclusion from school: a systematic approach. [electronic resource] [Online]. London: University of London.

Ricoeur, P. 1978. The philosophy of Paul Ricoeur: An anthology of his work, Boston, Beacon Pr.

Riessman, C. K. 2008. Narrative methods for the human sciences, London, SAGE.

Roberts, B. 2002. Biographical research, Buckingham, Open University Press.

Robson, C. 2002. Real world research: a resource for social scientists and practitioner-researchers, Oxford, Blackwell Publishers.

Roffey, S. & O'Reirdan, T. 2003. Plans for better behaviour in the primary school: management and intervention, London, David Fulton.

Rogers, B. 2005. How to manage children's challenging behaviour, London, Sage.

Rogers, B. 2015. Classroom behaviour: a practical guide to effective teaching, behaviour management and colleague support, London, Sage.

Rogers, J. A. 2005. The perspectives of pupils with specific learning difficulties (dyslexia) on the nature of the educational provision they receive in mainstream school. Leeds: University of Leeds.

Rogers, P. 2006. Youth, urban management & public space: reconciling social exclusion and urban renaissance. Newcastle upon Tyne press: University of Newcastle upon Tyne.

Roth, I., Barson, C., Hoekstra, R., Pasco, G. & Whatson, T. 2010. The autism spectrum in the 21st century: exploring psychology, biology and practice, London, Jessica Kingsley.

Rowley, J. 2009. School Exclusions. Shropshire Children and Young People's Services Scrutiny Panel.

Ruddock, A. & Mc Intyre, J. 2007. Investigating audiences, London, Sage.

Rudduck, J. & McIntyre, D. 2007. Improving learning through consulting pupils, London, Routledge.

Ruebain, D. 1994. Code of practice on procedure: admissions, exclusions, reinstatements: county, voluntary and maintained special school appeals, Association of Metropolitan Authorities.

Ryan, J. O. 2006. Inclusive leadership, Chichester, John Wiley.

Sapsford, R. & Jupp, V. 2008. Data collection and analysis, London, Sage.

Sayed, Y. 2007. Education exclusion and inclusion - policy and implementation in South Africa and India, London, Department for International Development.

Schratz, M. & Walker, R. 1995. Research as social change: new opportunities for qualitative research, London, Routledge.

Schunk, D. H., Pintrich, P. R. & Meece, J. L. 2010. Motivation in education: theory, research, and applications, London, Pearson Education.

Scott, D. & Usher, R. 1996. Understanding educational research, London, Routledge.

Searle, C. 2001. An exclusive education: race, class and exclusion in British schools, London, Lawrence & Wishart.

Sharp, J., Ward, S. & Hankin, L. 2009. Education studies: an issues-based approach, Exeter, Learning Matters.

Shevlin, M. & Rose, R. 2003. Encouraging voices: respecting the insights of young people who have been marginalised, Dublin, NDA.

Sikes, P. & Gale, K. 2006. Narrative Approaches to Education Research [Online]. Plymouth: University of Plymouth.

Silverman, D. 2009. Doing qualitative research: a practical handbook, London, Sage.

Simons, M. 2010. An Elicitation of Students' Perspectives on Exclusion and PRU Provision in Two Pupil Referral Units in the South of England (Book One); An Exploration of the Factors Affecting the Reintegration of Excluded Pupils into Mainstream Schools http://www.tandfonline.com/doi/abs/10.1080/13632752.2012.706905 Exeter: University of Exeter.

Simpson, M. & Ure, J. 1994. Studies of differentiation practices in primary and secondary schools, Great Britain, Scottish Office, Research and Intelligence Unit.

Skiba, R. & Noam, G. G. 2001. Zero tolerance: can suspension and expulsion keep schools safe? San Francisco, Jossey-Bass.

Skidmore, D. 2004. Inclusion: the dynamic of school development, Buckingham, Open University Press.

Slee, R. 2011. He irregular school: exclusion, schooling, and inclusive education, New York, Routledge.

Smith, R. 1998. No lessons learnt: a survey of school exclusions, London, Church of England, Children's Society.

Sosa, E., Villanueva, E. & Brogaard, B. 2011. The epistemology of perception, Boston, Blackwell.

Stake, R. E. 2006. Multiple case study analysis, London, Guilford press.

Stanley, L. 1992. The auto/biographical: theory and practice of feminist autobiography, Manchester, Manchester University Press.

Steer, A. 2009. Learning behaviour: lessons learned: a review of behaviour standards and practices in our schools, Nottingham, DCSF Publications.

Suter, W. N. 2012. Introduction to educational research: a critical thinking approach, Thousand Oaks, Sage Publications, Inc.

Sutton, J. & Stewart, W. 2011. Learning to counsel: develop the skills, insight and knowledge to counsel others, Oxford, How To Books.

Taylor, C. 2005. Young people in care and criminal behaviour, Philadelphia, Jessica Kingsley Publishers.

Thambirajah, M. S., Grandison, K. J. & De-Hayes, L. 2008. Understanding school refusal: a handbook for professionals in education, health and social care, London, Jessica Kingsley.

Thomas, G. & Pring, R. 2004. Evidence-based practice in education, Maidenhead, Open University Press.

Thompson, J. D. (ed.) 2010. Understanding Special Educational Needs, Gosport, Hants: Ashford Colour Press.

Thorsdottir, F. 2005. On the validity of attitude measurements in survey research: a comparison of psychometric models https://www.ncbi.nlm.nih.gov/pmc/articles/PMC3846512/ London: University of London.

Tod, J. & Blamires, M. 1999. Individual Education Plans. Speech and language, London, David Fulton.

Tough, J. 1976. Listening to children talking: a guide to the appraisal of children's use of language, Ward Lock Educational.

Travers, C. J. & Cooper, C. L. 2006. Teachers under pressure: stress in the teaching profession, London, Routledge.

Trust, T. L. 2004. Behaviour Support Plan. London, Hackney County Hall.

Turner, C. 2011. Supporting children with learning difficulties: holistic solutions for severe, profound and multiple disabilities, London, Continuum. University, C. 2011. Exclusion of Pupils London.

Author. 2009. Special needs children excluded eight times more often. The Guardian

Verhoeven, P. S. 2012. Doing research: the hows and whys of applied research, Chicago, Ill., Lyceum Books.

Walker, I. R. 2011. Reliability in scientific research: improving the dependability of measurements, calculations, equipment, and software, Cambridge, Cambridge University Press.

Wallace, S. & Gravells, J. 2007. Mentoring, Exeter, Learning Matters.

Warnock, M. 1978. Special Educational Needs. Report of the Committee of Enquiry into the Education of Handicapped Children and Young People London: Her Majesty's Stationery Office.

Warnock, M. 2005. Special educational needs: a new look, Keele, Philosophy of Education Society of Great Britain.

Wearmouth, J., Glynn, T. & Berryman, M. 2005. Perspectives on student behaviour in schools: exploring theory and developing practice, London, Routledge.

Weale, S. 2016. School exclusions data in England only 'the tip of the iceberg' https://www.theguardian.com/education/2017/oct/10/school-exclusion-figures-date-england-only-tip-iceberg

Web, H. 2009. Fixed period exclusions. Winchester: Hampshire County Council.

Webster, L. & Mertova, P. 2007. Using narrative inquiry as a research method : an introduction to using critical event narrative analysis in research on learning and teaching, London, Routledge.

Weller, S. C. & Romney, A. K. 1988. Systematic data collection, Sage.

Wheelock, V. 2007. Healthy eating in schools: a handbook of practical case studies, Skipton, Verner Wheelock.

Wilson, D. 2005. Using solution focused brief therapy to support secondary aged pupils facing exclusion from school [Online]. Newcastle upon Tyne: University of Newcastle upon Tyne.

Wilson, E. 2010. School-based research: a guide for education students, London, Sage.

Wise, S. (ed.) 2007. Listen to Me! The Voices of pupils with emotional and behavioural difficulties. London, Chapman publishing.

Woodbridge, M. W. & Sumi, W. C. 2009. Implementing evidence-based interventions in elementary schools for students with and at-risk for severe behaviour disorders, London, Sage.

Wright, C., Weekes-Barnard, D. & McGlaughlin, A. 2000. "Race," class, and gender in exclusion from school, London, Falmer Press.

Wright, C. T. H., Standen, P., John, G., German, G. & Patel, T. (eds.) 2005. School exclusion and transition into adulthood in African - Caribbean communities. York, Joseph Rowntree Foundation.

Yin, R. K. 2009. Case study research : design and methods, London, Sage.

Young, P. & Tyre, C. 1983. Dyslexia or illiteracy? Realising the right to read, Milton Keynes, Open University Press.

Yu, G. & Thomas, S. D. 2008. Research project - school effectiveness and education quality in Southern and East Africa : the range and extent of school effects in SACMEQ II school systems, Bristol, EdQual.

Zinn, J. 2004. Social Contexts and Responses to Risk Network (SCARR). School of Social Policy, Sociology and Social Research (SSPSSR), University of Kent, Canterbury.

Index